By the same

Paul Ray at the Hospital a Picture of L
Student Life Cloth, 8vo, 6s (By Subscription

Pictures of East Anglian Life Foli
with 32 Photo-Etchings and 15 small Illustrations. *..... Luxe*, limited to 75 numbered copies, £7, 7s, all sold Ordinary Edition, limited to 500 copies, £5, 5s, twenty left All plates destroyed

Pictures from Life in Field and Fen Folio. Being 20 Photo Etchings, with Introductory Essay, in Portfolio *Edition de Luxe*, limited to 50 numbered copies, £5, 5s Ordinary Edition, limited to 200 copies, £1, 2s., three left All plates destroyed

Idyls of the Norfolk Broads Being 12 Autogravures, with Introductory Essay and Notes, in Portfolio *Edition de Luxe*, limited to 100 copies, £1, 11s 6d Ordinary Edition, limited to 100 copies, £1, 1s All plates destroyed

English Idyls Post 8vo, small Cloth, 2s. Second Edition

Wild Life on a Tidal Water. Illustrated with 30 Photogravures *Edition de Luxe*, limited to 100 numbered copies, £3, 3s Ordinary Edition, limited to 300 numbered copies, £1, 1s All plates destroyed

Naturalistic Photography. Third Edition. (*In the Press*)

Nature Stories, Myths and Phantasies Cloth, 8vo, 1s ('Young Pan') Out of Print

East Coast Yarns. Paper Boards, 1s

A Son of the Fens Cloth, 8vo, 6s

Signor Lippo . Burnt cork Artiste 8vo, stiff paper covers, 1s

On English Lagoons Medium 8vo, Cloth, Illustrated, 7s 6d *Edition de Luxe*, with 15 Photogravures, numbered and limited to 100 copies Price £1, 5s All plates destroyed

Welsh Fairy Tales and other Stories Crown 8vo, Boards, 2s

Tales from Welsh Wales Crown 8vo, Fancy Cloth, 3s 6d

Birds, Beasts and Fishes of the Norfolk Broadland
Illustrated with 18 full page plates and 50 smaller Illustrations Medium 8vo, Cloth, 12s 6d Second Edition

JOINT AUTHOR OF

Life and Landscape on the Norfolk Broads Folio
Illustrated with 40 plates *Edition de Luxe*, limited to 25 copies, £10, 10s Ordinary Edition, limited to 175 copies, £6, 6s, a few left

Perspective Drawing and Vision Paper cover, 6d
Out of print

Marsh leaves

P H. 1856-1936 Emerson

MARSH LEAVES

MARSH LEAVE

BY

P. H. EMERSON

WITH

SIXTEEN PHOTO-ETCHINGS

FROM PLATES TAKEN BY

THE AUTHOR

'She shall wreathe them in shackles,
Shall weave them in fetters.'

TO

MY FRIEND AND

PUBLISHER

ALFRED NUTT

CONTENTS

		PAGE
I. OLD WROTE,		1
II. THE FENMAN'S CLOCK,		5
III. A DIKE FIRE,		8
IV. A MOONLIT MIDNIGHT,		11
V. MARSH CATS,		13
VI. LILAC AND GREEN,		20
VII. THE TOWN MOUSE AND THE COUNTRY MOUSE,		22
VIII. ON THE SANDHILLS,		26
IX. A BRAVE MARE,		29
X. BLACK AND GOLD,		32
XI BROADSMEN'S FROLICS,		34
XII. FIRST VOICE OF SPRING,		42
XIII. A HORSE-DEALER'S DEATH—LAST WISH,		44
XIV. A STUDY IN GOLD AND BLUE,		46
XV. COUNTRY COCKNEYS,		48
XVI. BIRD'S SLEEP,		50
XVII. VISIONS,		52
XVIII. CUCKOO-TIME,		56
XIX. FINE LADIES,		58
XX. GROWING WEATHER,		62
XXI. DROPPED EGGS,		64
XXII. GOLD AND BRONZE,		65
XXIII. CONSCIENCE MUCK-RAKE,		66
XXIV. A NIGHT-WALK IN EARLY SPRING,		67
XXV. A SAD DOCUMENT		69
XXVI. A LANDSCAPE,		71
XXVII. THE TWO WAYS,		73
XXVIII. RETURN OF SPRING,		75

CONTENTS

		PAGE
XXX.	THE STRAY TURTLE-DOVE,	79
XXXI	THE MAY MOON,	81
XXXII	THE WAYS OF WOMAN,	84
XXXIII.	YOUNG LIFE,	87
XXXIV	BLACKTHORN WINTER,	90
XXXV	A LITTLE LEARNING IS A DANGEROUS THING,	92
XXXVI	THE COCK AND HEN,	95
XXXVII.	VOICES OF THE NIGHT,	97
XXXVIII	A GOOD DINNER,	99
XXXIX	THE FIRST MARTIN,	102
XL.	A WHERRYMAN—HIS WATCH,	103
XLI	A QUIET AFTERNOON,	104
XLII	AT A MARSH INN,	106
XLIII	ON THE STUBBLE,	109
XLIV	A NOCTURNE,	111
XLV	A NORTHERLY BREEZE,	114
XLVI	THE NEW WHERRYMAN,	116
XLVII	THE TIDE-PULSE,	120
XLVIII	RURAL FELICITY,	125
XLIX	THE VILLAGE BIRD-STUFFER,	127
L.	SUNDAY AFTERNOON,	129
LI	THE BEWITCHED PIG,	131
LII	THE WIND AGAINST THE LAW,	132
LIII	A COUNTRY CHILD,	134
LIV	A DAY WITH THE RATS,	137
LV	COTTAGE PROPERTY,	141
LVI.	LOVE-TIME,	143
LVII	THREE WRECKERS,	144
LVIII	BLUE, AMBER, AND GREEN,	145
LIX	THE IRISH STEER,	147
LX	THE SPIDER AND THE FLIES,	150
LXI	RAIN AND MELANCHOLY,	152
LXII	OLD BEWTIES,	154
LXIII	THE VOICES OF THE REED,	157
LXIV	A MAY MORNING,	160
LXV	POLLY'S VALENTINE,	163

LIST OF PLATES

E

A WINTER'S SUNRISE, . . *Frontispiece.*

THE LONE LAGOON, *To face page* 11

THE FETTERS OF WINTER, . „ 20

A WATERSIDE INN, „ 34

A WINTER PASTORAL, . . „ 46

MARSH WEEDS, . „ 56

GNARLED THORN-TREES, „ 62

THE MISTY RIVER, „ 75

BLEAK WINTER, „ 90

THE WAKING RIVER, „ 102

THE BRIDGE, „ 111

THE SNOW GARDEN, . „ 125

A CORNER OF THE FARM-YARD, . „ 131

RIME CRYSTALS, . „ 143

THE LONELY FISHER, . . . „ 152

THE LAST GATE, . . „ 160

' We slip the world's grey husk,
  Emerge and spread new plumes
  In sunbeam-fretted dusk,
  Through pop'lous golden glooms '
                    C F D Roberts, *On the Creek*

I

reed-cutter

OLD WROTE

'HE is always wroting about—no matter whether there be ice or sun—he's always wroting about—nothing riffles him,' the amphibian said, when the stoutly-built, bent old hulk of a man—now in his eighty-fourth year—walked slowly past supporting his huge torso on a stout ash stick.

Forty years ago Old Wrote was a six-foot man with ginger hair and blue eyes, and then he was the champion wrestler of the fen-lands; but even he did not escape the fierce shin-kicking matches, for his legs were notched and ridged like a rope-worn timber-head.

I saw this old man cutting stuff, wading clumsily about through the thin ice on the marsh, one cold winter day when the nor'-easter blew keenly from the sea. His big boots crashed through the ice and splashed up the mud as he waded from hillock to hillock cutting a forkful of stuff here and a forkful there.

I saw him again the following spring on the yellow reed-rond, with one of his giant sons, poling out a few fathoms of dry reed to his marsh-boat and talking aloud—for none spoke to him, he was as deaf as a post on the marshes. But he was always talking about 'wroting' and 'sixty years ago.'

As he helped load the boat he said, in his slow bass voice, 'Ha dar bor! I come at the wrong time,' and he snuffled thrice; 'work was scarce forty year ago, and flour four shillun a stone. Ha dar bor! used to get one and nine-pence for mowing an acre of grain in those days, and now you get three shillun. Ha, dar! used to eat turnips and sharps then'

He saw his son's lips move but heard nothing, and again he snuffled; then he continued:—

'Ha dar bor! bad times then; used to get eighteenpence for boating stuff, and now you, boy, get three shillun—good times now,' emphasising his speech with three defiant snuffles

The giant ginger-headed son made a grimace

'Ha dar bor! yes, good times now,' repeated Old Wrote, 'plenty of beer now. I could drink a pailful then, but that's too much now. Haugh!' and he snuffled a long, deep snuff of air.

The son smiled

'Haugh! I could; and I never let the sun get the master of me neither. But men were men then: we used to bend our backs like a rainbow at work, but now lots of 'em can't neither eat, drink, nor yet wrote.'

When the flat, black-pitched boat was loaded with reed-shooves, Old Wrote sat down under the lee in the bright sunshine and fell on his meat and bread—his fifth meal that day, for he ate his eight meals a day even now, and drank his beer with many of the younger generation. As he ate and drank he snuffled fiercely, and watched his son cutting a splinter from his hand.

'Dar bor! a shiver in the hand; mean, you don't wrote'; for this hardy but deaf old Hercules despised the young men of the day, saying they were more like 'mawthers' with their prayer-meetings, smooth tongues, and lazy ways.

. . I heard afterwards Old Wrote had, by dint of hard work, kept a little farm going until he was sixty-eight, when the times mastered him and he had to give up, after which he hired the finest slips of ragged land-ronds, hanging to the river walls, farming the rough crops of rush and reed growing thereon to provide for his simple wants.

Whilst at this work he did not deign even to answer the young men, but when he saw a good workman he would always stop and speak to him.

One starry February morning he came steering along the river through the thick mists soon after daybreak, when most of the young men lay abed afraid of getting influenza, which was raging in the village; but presently he came upon a young marshman who feared nothing, and was at work in the fog cutting rushes.

Old Wrote stopped his marsh-boat.

'Rather thick morning,' shouted the marshman, straightening himself.

'Ay, bor, that it is,' said the old man in his deep bass voice.

'It's rather unhealthy morning.'

'Ay, damn you, them reeks won't hurt you—you keep on wroting, put that old scythe into it, you'll be allright'; and he shoved off to his own wroting—cutting reed.

But at times, much as he loved wroting, he felt that his path was not the most profitable, and one day when three of the villagers lay dead of influenza his sons told him they were tolling the *little* church bell.

'Haugh, damn bor! they're cleverer in the skull than we are; they don't like to get hold of much hard work, they know too much to ring the *big* bell.'

On this particular morning, as the old man and his giant son navigated a light load down the blue winding river, I could not but feel the men of those days were giants; and as I saw the bent figure of the old man handling his pole surely and effectively at eighty-four, and when I thought of the pailfuls of beer, and how he had sown his fields of corn and herded his herds of pigs, and fought and lived and worked so that he had become known only by the name of 'Old Wrote,' or 'Old Worker,' I marvelled.

The only regret—it was no whine—that ever escaped those manly lips was that he was born at the wrong time. 'Work was better paid now,' he said, and he continued making plans for work ten and twenty years ahead.

II

THE FENMAN'S CLOCK

HE was a tall, raw-boned man with the curious jumping walk of the true-bred fenman—a gait acquired in walking hastily over quaking bogs and floating hovers, and the fenman's lithe swinging arms, a motion acquired by swinging the scythe over miles of rushy marshland and shoving his flat marsh-boat along in the face of stiff gales as deftly as when nothing but a breeze ruffles the surface of the water. He'd the keen fenman's eye for wild-birds' eggs —a black fine eye that roamed to the blue misty horizon of his wide breezy domain. His ear was quick as a wild animal's, too, and he could tell the name of any bird after nightfall, and much of the gossip that the old women talked when they weeded in the springtime within the brightly-flowering hawthorn hedges, where the green linnets nested and whistled softly.

But with all his accomplishments his fingers were 'numb' when it came to delicate work. Still that did not deter him from taking his clock to pieces one day when she was out of order. There he was in his cottage, his table covered with wheels and screws. As I asked him how he got on with his self-imposed task, he exclaimed, ' Ay, bor, I onscrewed her and took her works out, and then I got the brush what Jenny sweep up the house with and brushed the wheels, but I didn't take stock where I got the wheels from, for I laid 'em all among the other.'

And he began clumsily putting them in anywhere he could: some he fixed in holes where they touched empty spaces, but they were all finally packed in somehow, and after the face and back weie applied he hung the clock up, and behold! it moved.

But in the fulness of time he found that his old clock went two hours to one of any other clock. However, she lasted till his wife broke the spring one night when she viciously wound up the irregular machine, for the old clock with the painted ship on red waves resented hei force, there was a whirr, and the broken spring uncuiled and lay limp in the case. Yet the fenman was in no way disheartened.

He took the works out as before, and taking the mainspring and a bolt he heated the spring to a red glow, and bending it to the bolt, as he would a willow wand for trapping moles, he secured it with a crooked piece of wire gathered from a ' pop bottle.' Or, as he said himself—

' I stopped the end back so that didn't ondo. When I got the gripe onto her, then I shipped her and sciewed her in, an' away she go ; but she wanted a lot o' winding up arter that, so I took her to the clockmakers' and they set her right, and she runned all right for two year, when she got grimy and wouldn't keep time; but I soon found the best way to clean her, and I allus do that every year now.

'When she's dirty I takes her works out and biles 'em in the saucepan for an hour; then I stands 'em on the hob to dry, and arter that I grease with paraffin, and she do go right beautiful   Look at her.'

And the clock struck all it could in vindication of the cleaner.

III

A DIKE FIRE

COOL southerly wind breathed over the frost-sered marsh grasses, tossing the yellowing reed-stalks against the azure, and creaking the dried stalks of the water-plants, or caressing the feathery blooms of the colt's-foot and the yellow enamelled patches of kingcups blazing by the dike-side in the white sunlight, when with roar and crackle the fat, powdery, gladen stalks growing in tangled masses in a neglected dike burst into a sheet of flame, one long, lambent tongue of flickering fire rising from a blue, vapoury mist, and filling the ambient air with a delicate fragrance of charred flowers, as with fiery tongues of passion the fire leaped into the sombre smoke-clouds and palpitating, glassy heat-waves floating over it like a nimbus. Fading, dying down, and leaping up into a roar in the waywardness of passion at red heat, the long dike burned, but even in its strongest gusts dark lines streaked the pure flame when the charred stems of the water-plants had burnt themselves out: the fingers of Death were already upon the merry fire.

And the quiet marshland life looked on with desire, for

the quickly leaping flames and drifting smoke fascinated from afar the herds, and men shouted with quick, eager voices, for the spirit of contention floated into their bosoms, and all the madness of a fierce passion spending itself was in the air

As the fire burned out, leaving heated embers and hot ashes, the sun burnt more fiercely, and the frost-burnt grasses looked greener by the hot breath of the glowing fire, even the dark-skinned frogs had crept from their slimy beds and crooned their noontide lullaby, reposing in the hot air upon soft beds of dead and sodden water-plants, while some, more amorous, embraced in the warm waters of the dike, and rolled clumsily about as they were pushed aside by some frolicsome pike that sported with warmth and love over some water-weeds.

Even the breath of the landscape was delicately scented with a watery perfume, instilling soft desire into the heart of man, and even into the watery tribe of birds, for all around through the warm air resounded the voices of burning love Snipe drummed overhead, redshanks whistled plaintively to their mates, larks rose on fluttering wings, singing before the hens lapwings sported and played in the air crying their passionate notes, and a sweet-voiced woman sang a love-song softly, as she hung her lover's shirts to dry in the bright sunlight, the ringdove in the wood took up her soft crooning, and the passionate turkey-cock crowed to his harem. All life was throbbing with life and love, for the subtle influence of the springtide thrilled the blood and brightened the eye Little they recked that love and life, like the red-flamed tongues, must fade. They were wiser than man cursed with the gift of pale thought; they loved fiercely and lived hotly while the springtide was fair. They no more than the ruddy flames whined and paled because their passion must die; their energy was spent in living and doing, and the ashes of such living furnaces shall be as the ashes of the water-plants, a rich and rare remains of the sane and brave in heart, for the breath of passion lasteth for ever, and the fires spent to-day breathe into lives unborn a virtue more precious than all the thought of ages,—in sooth, the principal *blessing*, that man should go down and love and live, and wrestle and die

IV

A MOONLIT MIDNIGHT

T seemed as though night had fallen and a sober day was born, as the bright moon lit up the grey-green landscape and awoke the birds, for the air was alive with their cries.

From afar sounded the laughing of snipe, the chatter of reed- and sedge-warblers, the ticking of the shy grasshopper-warbler, and the short, sweet note of reed-bunting and yellow wagtail, whilst away down the ronds of the dusky river a water-rail was twanging the monotonous *ting-ting-ting*, increasing from a slow voice to a crescendo, followed by a pause —she probably had her young brood about her. All through the desultory clamourings of the marsh birds she twanged without ever a pause, perfectly undisturbed by even the shrill whistling of redshanks.

But all these voices seemed to come from afar, and to be an undertone to the hilarious cries of the wheeling cock-lapwings that were at times answered by the sad voices of the hen. All about in the moonlight their white glancing wings gleamed as they shrieked more softly than is their wont by day their curious cry, 'T'ree bullocks a week, week arter week, week arter week.' All the air was vibrant with their voices, and they grew so eager and excited in their cries that they seemed to speak—their voices took a human interest, so earnest was their tone. Indeed, I think they were directing the hen-birds with the young from their cradles in the rushy marsh to the water, and upon such journeyings it is usual for the males to fly overhead, wheeling and crying, guiding their little families over to the grey waters, where they shall learn to feed and bathe; for the lapwing is a cleanly bird, and poetic, loving to bathe his green crest when the bright moon silvers the mist hanging over river and marsh.

And as the stars brightened, towards the dawn, and the mere began to pale, I left the misty, moonlit scene, with the memory of glancing white wings and the earnest voice of the bird of the moonlight—the crested lapwing.

V

MARSH CATS

MUCH has been written in praise of the cat. The bright side of that soft, effeminate animal, filled with deceit, has been given. It may be because I detest the soft, purring, cunning character of the cat that I determined to watch it when not pampered on rugs or upon the soft materials of ladies' dresses, for the wild state shows your beast's true nature.

I wandered, then, down by a little farm on the marsh-lands, just within the jagged fortalice of the marram-bound dunes, and there the dreadful little beast's ways were un-masked. I had previously observed his unmannish love of warmth, good food, and 'cultured' society. I had noticed pussy's admirers were women, or barren males. I had felt my terrier's innate dislike of the respectable creature was well founded; for he is a good fellow, my terrier—no deceit, no duplicity, and he loves a brawl and a flirtation with any terrier—but he is not 'respectable.' But to return to my studies.

The feminine portion of the little farmer's family kept five cats : think of it. They pleaded, in a cattish way, 'mice' as an excuse for their pets, and their pets pleaded 'affection' as an excuse for their poaching 'You could see their souls in their eyes,' the girls said ; and, of course, they knew. And have not some writers written eloquently (and foolishly) of their souls ?

Well, well, I watched first at dawn, before the sun rose over the budding osier cars, and I watched after the light of day had faded from the landscape, and left the marshland to the cats and to me.

At such half-lit seasons the ladies and the cats drew forth quietly along the hedgerows Eva and Florrie and Gertie to meet their lovers, and the sandy and the tortoise-shell and the light cyprus and the dark cyprus to poach— they met their lovers later on The white cat alone, I deemed, was no poacher. I found afterwards that white cats are too intellectual to poach, but not a whit more honest than these born poachers the sandy, tortoiseshell, and cyprus cats. I picked upon the sandy cat and followed her as she crept along the hedgerows, now green with young hawthorn leaves I watched her stop at times and sit down to listen —her head raised, ears erect, and tail curled round her, its end flicking nervously Anon away she crept along and through hedgerows, going on a poaching cat-line for half a mile to the 'strong eyes' at the foot of the sandhills, as the rabbits' 'burghs' or burrows are picturesquely called in the marshland. The roar of the sea in the still gloaming drowned the noise of my clumsy steps. I lay down behind the green marram-crested tussock, where the leaves of the silver-weed mixed with the sandy crop, and I watched my sandy lady. As she neared the burgh the sentinel rabbit tapped the hollow, dry ground quickly with his hind feet—their usual danger-signal—and every bunny sat up on end, threw back his long ears, and looked for his particular 'eye'; indeed, all the bank seemed to be suddenly turned into eyes, dotted with white tails But pussy was too quick for a young but well-grown rabbit. She sprang upon it, seized it by the side of the neck, and these two furry creatures lay on their sides struggling to the music of the sea. Pussy—the quiet, cultured creature with a soul—was busily hammering the defenceless and inexperienced rabbit to death in a truly feline and feminine manner with her hind feet, their usual method, I soon found, of killing rabbits and young hares

Presently young bunny expired, her eyes looking into the sentinel stars that began to shine more brightly in the violet sky, and pussy began quietly to eat her prey, beginning at the head and working towards the shoulders.

After a time I learned that pussy could turn a bunny out of its skin as cleverly as a taxidermist.

When pussy had eaten her fill, she dragged the carcass to an islet of bramble and jogged off home, looking as innocent as any other soulful criminal, and as determined as any 'reformed' cut-throat to return to her mangled carcass the next evening, after the larks had dropped to their warm beds in the dry tufts of grass, and so on until not a vestige remained.

As I soon found, many of the amphibians had a just appreciation of pussy, and rated her as the biggest poacher about the marshland, and many had known her to bring home full-grown rabbits, and even half-grown hares, to her kittens.

It was well known, too, that if pussy discovered a nest of young rabbits she could never rest until she had killed and eaten every suckling Nor is pussy always so careful of appearances as Eva and Florrie and Gertie. She at times commits her excesses in the full glare of the sun, as indeed, after all, do some Evas, but that is a gentleman's story, and when the good old Greek dinner customs return I will tell it you

But we must not forget the white cat, the intellectual animal who would not poach, but would follow her master about like a dog, and turn her yearning eyes up to her master's when he aimed at a speckled mavish or a noisy black-bird. Ere the smoke had cleared away white puss was off after the fallen bird in her ladylike way, and having captured it, unlike a dog, she would gallop off home with it, to mangle and eat in her own particular way

Puss has not sufficient gratitude to retrieve, though the girls think that she might be taught, but, like women, the poor cats are so down-trodden by the superior race—dog.

In sooth, any cat, except a gelding, will, on occasion, poach, especially if not too highly fed ; and once they begin to poach, Florrie can no longer plead 'mice,' for from that day they will never disturb a mouse in the house. Moreover, they will often go off and breed in rabbit-holes, in thorn-stacks, or in plantings, with their prey within easy reach, and such cats are the rabbits' most deadly enemies, for they so much resemble a rabbit—especially in the half lights—that they have but little difficulty in catching their prey.

I know a marshman who once saw a hare crossing a field at night, and the following night he determined to lay wait for 'Sarah'; so he hid himself in a ditch by the roadway, where he knew the old hare would be sure to come after traversing the field. As he anticipated, his prey came across the field, but stopped: 'It smelt a rat!' Instantly he fired, and on running forward to pick up his booty he found a 'big, old, sondy cat'

A friendly poacher will often tell you he has been dis-appointed by finding cats in his snares, and he will dwell with the gusto of a Chinese gourmet on the size and plumpness of the wild 'escapes' he has at times taken when brushing a snared planting for hares. Sometimes he finds the whelps, and he will tell you the young will spit and raise their hair on end at you

I remember an old fenman who once nearly got into trouble for shooting a cat-poacher.

A large tortoiseshell cat frequented Farmer Howard's 'strong eyes,' and played havoc amongst the rabbits, for all hands were too busy to do anything but harvest the golden corn. However, when harvest was over, and the largars feast had been held, old Bob was told off to kill the poacher.

Practised as he was in the art of trapping, he set the steel-
fall baited with bloater, and next morning the tortoiseshell
cat was caught by one leg, and as Bob with his gun came
stealing towards her, puss threw herself about and pulled
her foot off, then went limping off towards her hole, but the
report of Bob's gun sounded across the silent marshes and
poor pussy's thieving-days were over, and her body thrown
into a ditch to wither like the corpses of criminals in olden
days.   The owner heard of the matter, and 'pulled' Bob for
maliciously killing his cat   Bob, a truthful man, owned he
had killed the cat, but denied malice.   The vicious owner
could find no witnesses of the murder, the case was adjourned
for a fortnight, and finally the owner of the dear pet ate
humble-pie, made friends with Bob, and paid all expenses
incidental to the business.

   Old Bob, like myself, is no lover of cats; he will allow
them no virtues, and maintains strongly that even their
reputation for having nine lives is a great exaggeration,
averring that, in this respect, the ferret tribe must take
precedence of the cat.

   'Well, bor,' said Bob, smoking at his short, black pipe,
'last winter-time I'd a ferret what was no good, and I wanted
to kill that   The broad was laid, people was skating over
it, and the ground was froze hard as a rock.   So I got this
here ferret on to the hard ground in my garden by the broad,
and I hit him with the flat of the spade all my might, and
his feet spread out, and he gaped, and I thowt him dead, so
I hulled him onter the ice and went indoors   Two days

arterwards I went to feed my ferrets,—I 'd shot some sparrows for 'em,—and blow me if that there warmin what I 'd killed didn't pop out under the tub and commence to eat away with the rest. Thinks I, I 'll kill you agin, so I got the spade and flattened him out till his eyes started from his head and his chops frothed and runned blood, then I hulled him onter the ice agin. Now, blow me, as I start watching on him, if he didn't get up and begin running on the ice. That was no use hitting on him, I couldn't kill him, so I drowned him. Now, bor, no cat alive would have stood that!'

VI

LILAC AND GREEN

FOR five days and five nights boisterous nor'-easters or nor'-westers had blown over the face of the marshland, blowing the clear waters into many-coloured ripples on the shallows; for the fierce breath of the wind discovered the many-coloured floors of the shallow—red clay, bice green, and the darker hue of the hair-weed. But at last the gale was over and the wind shifted to the sou'-west, and a pale lilac haze veiled the distant landscape and tinted the sky, on whose westerward horizon a light yellowish sun sank imperceptibly to rest, leaving the green marshlands with the lilac zone of trees and a low dome of a paler lilac, broken only in one patch—the pale yellow glory of the departed sun.

And in that peaceful eventide swallows played and twittered over the red chimney-tops, cuckoos called sleepily, and redshanks, pink of ear, for their young, piped mournfully as the cattle-man followed the homing cows, crying, 'Come along, co—co—co—c—o'; again, 'Come along, co—co—co —co'

The light sou'-westerly breeze died away with the sun; the mill-sails slept in the lilac sky, and all Nature seemed in a trance right up to the green-chequered sandhills, beyond which the sea fretted with hoarse voice along the shifting sea-beach, crooning lullabies to the sitting ring-dotterel and pied oyster-catchers.

As the blue deepened in tint a silvery pike jumped in the river, and the dark-furred water-vole came forth to feed on the newly-grown shoots of the sedge.

The last voice to be heard was that of the lilac bird—the cuckoo—on the green banks

VII

THE TOWN MOUSE AND THE COUNTRY MOUSE

E was a stout, alert, quick, business man, who had hired the gunner from his marshes to help him move into his newly acquired cottage on the borders of a sluggish river watering the marshland.

Those twain were occupied a fortnight filling the cottage with furniture, and each day the stout, city-bred man chaffed the gunner with fine city words.

'You always see something to shoot when you han't a gun,' said he, pointing jeeringly at the village cat's-meat man, as he passed down the road.

'What, do he sell meat cheap like that?' asked the gunner.

'Yes, oh yes!' said the alert citizen, smiling; 'have a piece?'

The sordid vendor of dry meats was called, and the gunner bought and ate a couple of slices, and found it good, until he had swallowed the last mouthful, when the hearty citizen said—

The following autumn the jovial citizen asked the gunner to show him some fowl.

'Yes, bor,' said the gunner.

And they went on the marshes, for the citizen was a quick shot, he had learned snipe-shooting round the much-frequented drainage farms outside of London   But the acute marshman remembered the cat's-meat, and walked the jovial citizen into a bog up to his neck, and he laughed heartily, calling, 'Cat's meat,' as the citizen tried to extricate himself.

'Well, now,' said the citizen, 'we are quits,' and he stooped to pick a mushroom. 'What a number of mushrooms!' he cried with delight.

'Ay, bor, they'll stop; but do you get home and change, or you'll get the screwmatics'

Next morning at daybreak the citizen crept from his bed and, hastily dressing, walked down to the marsh in the mists to gather a basketful of the succulent fungi; but look as he would, and walk as he would, never a mushroom could he see, nor yet could he find the broken stalks whence they had been picked—sharp-eyed though he was.

'Very strange, very strange,' he muttered, and he shivered with cold as the red disc of the sun rose in the grey sky above a bed of reeds growing round a windmill. He was contemplating the magic beauty of the great spaces of

marsh, decorated in one corner with a pretty, natural composition of reed-bed, windmill, and red ball of fire, when a
figure appeared, coming mysteriously through the mists,
looking grey, and without substance, as ghostlike as wreaths
of cloud trailing in the misty sky across the silent stars,
shimmering palely in the eternal blue. As the figure grew
darker and more solid the bewildered citizen recognised
the gunner Joe, who carried on his arm a basket half filled
with dewy, rough-skinned mushrooms. Joe stopped as he
saw the citizen, and exclaimed—

'Ay, master, you got here first this morning, but you
didn't pick 'em all, did you?'

'No, no, Joe, it's very strange, the marsh was full of
them yesterday.'

'Yes, when my nabs fell inter bog'

'Ay, Joe, but that's quits. Here's a piece of silver; tell
us how you got those mushrooms.'

'We know something, then, though we don't come
from London,' said Joe, quizzically

'Yes, Joe; it's the old story of the town mouse and
the country mouse.'

'Well, master, I'll show yow,' said Joe, as he held his
basket in one hand and went along, stooping about his
mysterious work as he ran, a shadowy thing under the lift-
ing mists, and kept plucking the white buttons from the
marsh. Yet never a plant could the amazed citizen see.

When the last shreds of mist had melted away before
the sun, as they walked home together, Joe explained—

'Ay, bor, when we find musheroons on the mash we cover them up with grass or cow-dung; they grow better like that, and nobody else don't find 'em.'

And the quick-witted citizen gazed thoughtfully before him.

VIII

ON THE SANDHILLS

HAD often wondered why that long chain of hills held such a charm.

I saw them one May day with a loom upon them, surrounded by the green marsh-land—a quaint gem set in a reposeful background—a natural vignette of bewitching and delicate beauty.

But that was not their only charm, for I felt if one but knew that beyond those sea-breeze sculptured hollows there stretched fields of marsh and cornland their never-ceasing charm would be departed, and one would come to look upon them as cumbersome—as harbours for conies, and a trysting-place for peasant lads and lasses.

But as I stood looking upon them from a field whence a hare had started and a man was harrowing the poor land, I could hear the cry of the sea and smell its salt breath, and then I knew the dunes were full of the everlasting ring of the sea, a monument of her changefulness, instability, and wanton form and conduct.—That was their other charm.

As the seas break upon the coast and eat the land, so

the crumbling dune, the sand-developed flora of silver-weed and thistles acting as postillions, moves in stealthily and eats the flat land As the sea is now smooth, now in curved hollows, now full of gloomy caverns and bright crests, so are the sandhills, as the nesting dotterels know full well. And like the sea, the sandy waves burst into powdery drops—for they twain are twins eternal—encroachers on the land.

I walked through the warrens tunnelled by rabbits and littered with wreckage left from some ill-fated vessel, and mounted the slippery ascent to the gap where the fishermen passed to their boats lying without the sandy fortalice, when I came full face with the sea and saw through the sand-coloured gap, as through a frame, the matchless green and pearly ocean wrapped in a grey mist—the waters edged with white ribbons of foam that faded away down the wet sea-beaches. And again I felt the character of this marshland scenery—a speck of interest floating in a field of sameness, a form of composition beloved by the artists of the Land of the Rising Sun

And I sat upon a piece of wreckage streaked with cracks and tunnelled with gloomy bolt-holes, all studded with bent and flake-rusty bolts, the windward hollows filled with blown sand, and listened to the two-voiced sea, the near irregular, splashing clamours of the foaming waves as they broke upon the shifting shore, and the distant deep-toned, regular hum of the working sea-bottom, a music steady and sure, sounding as if the pivot upon which the world spun round was grinding in its bearings out there beneath those green and pearly fields.

And the determined music lulled me to sleep in my bed
in the warm marram, till the white flakes of the breaking
waves flickered through the mist like the wings of sea-birds,
and the sandhills seemed to rise and fall; and once again
I felt that the sea and the dunes were one, indissolubly,
eternally united, until the mighty roar of the spinning
world shall cease for ever and ever.

IX

A BRAVE MARE

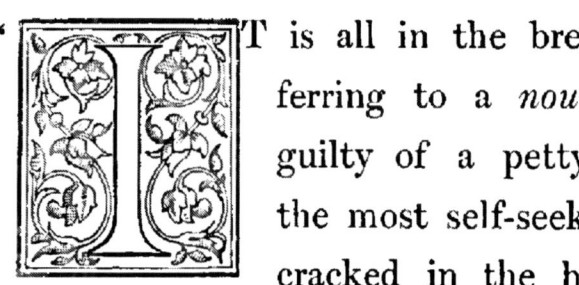'T is all in the breed,' said Lady Gussy, referring to a *nouveau riche* who had been guilty of a petty meanness, for such are the most self-seeking in the world. 'He's cracked in the heels,' continued her ladyship, with one of her archest looks and piquant expressions.

'And so it is all in the breed, for your well-bred un never gets the grease,' agreed an old warrior.

'It's all in the breed,' said the marsh farmer who owned the Irish steer, and so said the marsh farmer who owned the sturdy English mare.

There had been a thaw that February, but the wind had suddenly shifted to the nor'east, and a wind-frost had laid the mere and dikes with ice as thick as the farmer's middle finger was long, and had made the roads slippery as glass.

The marshman, however, went round with his coil of rope and dog in the cold February twilight to see if his six horses, feeding, tails to the wind, on the frozen marsh, were safe, and returned to his lone cottage shivering, for the nor'-

easter had freshened and brought snow-powder and hail-shot in the snow-squalls.

At daybreak the old man started again, under the light of the wintry stars, on his rounds over the marshes. As he walked by a trickling spring, a snipe flew up, scaping, and as his big boots crushed over the frozen marsh he started a lark from her warm form in the lee of a knob of rush. He recognised his horses by their steaming breath; they were all huddled together by the gateway, rubbing their shaggy coats against each other for warmth. But there were only five: Jinny, the big nine-year-old dark-bay brood mare—she was in foal, too—was missing. The old man looked over the dark levels, and began to follow the silvery line of the dike, walking along towards the river-wall, when suddenly the icy ice-way was broken by a dense, ill-shapen object. Approaching, he found Jinny in the dike, only her head, withers, and rump showing above the broken glaze and water. As he came up to her she placed her fore-feet on the ice, made a lunge forward, and began calmly to feed on the poor crop of grass growing on the bank. The old marshman saw she had broken her way some fifty yards through the thin ice, and already her jagged path through the glaze had frozen with a darker, thinner, more streaked ice, the shore too was closely cropped all along her track. As the old man called her affectionately, Jinny looked up in the dark, and then resumed her feed. The old man looked at his rope, but he knew his feeble strength could never drag that powerful mare from the icy slime, so he hurried home to the farm for help

Through numerous delays, the marshman, the farmer, and his man, with two powerful horses, did not reach Jinny before three o'clock in the afternoon, and though the biting nor'-easter was blowing and icy snow-squalls were passing over the face of the land, still Jinny only trembled and shivered. She had broken, however, through more than a hundred yards of ice, and had cropped all along the bank on her way.

The men dug an incline in the bank, and, putting the cart-rope round Jinny's neck, they twisted it up and tied a bow-line which they hooked to the horse-trace. Then the powerful horses were urged forward over the frozen marsh; stooping, straining, and slipping they plodded forward and drew the shivering Jinny from the mud and icy water.

Immediately the rope was removed from her neck Jinny stumbled to her feet, shook herself, stood trembling for a minute, and—began feeding, 'unconsarned as a passenger,' as the marshman remarked.

I saw her the day after, with her foal, both happy and healthy as the larks soaring above them.

X

BLACK AND GOLD

TOWARDS the evening of an April day the blue, hard sky, dried and polished by the easterly wind, grew pied around the horizon with dark, low-lying clouds, fantastic in shape, floating slowly and tranquilly across the arid sky, for the wind had gone to the north-east, whence come snow-squalls and icy hail.

As the sun sank below the dull green marshland, the clouds gathered all round the horizon, and all round the pale blue dome there seemed to rise from the marshes numberless tiny clouds, ill-shapen in form and frowning in mien, black, sluggish vapour — forms that later became edged with silver as the pale golden disc of the moon came from behind and peeped forth from between their ragged hollows.

Shortly they floated past the waning bright disc, flattened in its left cheek, oscillating as does the mimic landscape at the play.

When the clouds had passed, the moon floated clear in

all at once, in the silent night, the deep call of the water-hen resounded through the still, clear night air—that voice from the black bird with the wax-like crest—a sound as of the heart-beat of the silvery waters flowing sluggishly through the low marshlands.

XI

BROADSMEN'S FROLICS

VERY one of the amphibians is a small-boat sailor. You may see the boys at seven and eight sailing over the lagoon in an old coble with a bit of torn sail, navigating the rickety, leaky old craft with the science of a *voyageur*.

In this way they all get to love their boats, and the greatest blow the foreigner (from the adjoining villages) can strike at the waterside dwellers is to come with a boat and take all the prizes from the natives living on the reedy ronds and the water; nor must a foreigner have greater skill in sailing on the lagoon than a native. If he have, the amphibians will blush to the roots of their hair and avoid the subject as taboo, for their pride on such occasions is deeply hurt.

One fine morning in May a gentleman in his yacht sailed on to the lagoon, towing his little jolly behind him. The little craft was called *The Little Maid*. The owner was sportively inclined, so he arranged to sail a match against his sailing master, a native of the lagoon. A newly built

boat, much thought of by the amphibian, was selected to race *The Little Maid*

The little racer was taken from the reed-thatched boat-house, where a tomtit had already built its nest, drawn up to the staith, where the iron ballast was shipped, the yew-fir mast stepped, the sail bent to the big yards, and the boat made fit for the match. *The Young Rover* looked, and was, a bigger boat, longer by nearly two feet, but both carried about the same spread of canvas—well-set balance lug-sails.

After tossing for 'lays'—the course, about three miles in length, having been settled on—the broadsman, who had lost the toss, got into *The Little Maid,* and the amateur, whose watermanship was yet untried, took *The Young Rover* in hand A fine nor'-westerly breeze was blowing an ex-hilarating air, that made the cuckoos call loudly from the coppices as the old watermen assembled beneath the budding willows to watch the contest. There were some grumbling that the untried amateur should have to show *The Young Rover's* prowess against the experienced amphibian, who was accounted the cleverest small-boat sailor on the lagoon ; still the amateur was cool, and as the referee gave the word, 'Two rounds, and luff round all stakes except the first,' the competitors sailed up to the winning-post, and getting in line, the word was given, 'Off!'

Sheets well pulled in, and away they went down to the first stake with a three-quarters' wind, sitting their boats as steadily as a swan swims. Gradually *The Young Rover* drew ahead, and then the clever old sailor in *The Little*

Maid, ashamed to get alee the amateur, held his course, went round the first stake, pulling in his sheet and going away leading down to the second stake, three-quarters of a mile distant Directly *The Little Maid* turned the stake she shot up into the wind and away she darted, sailing closer than *The Rover,* whose straight, low lines and small tiller rendered her awkward to handle, for her sail could not be pulled in for fear of her filling—indeed, she had been turned over many a time However, the amateur held the lead to the second stake, and luffing round that, started away back, close-hauled, for the stake three-quarters of a mile off. But here *The Little Maid* proved her superiority : she kept luffing up to the wind, and shot ahead and reached the stake first, starting off to tack across to the starting-stake

As the two boats came tacking up to windward the amphibians swore terrible oaths They accused the amateur of knowing nothing about sailing, saying he didn't know one end of a boat from the other, he didn't let her go, he didn't know how to put a boat about, and so on

The amateur, however, held on, for he had long ago discovered his tiller was too small and his boat wouldn't handle , moreover, she was leaking, and would soon become water-logged

However, away they started on the second round; and finally *The Little Maid* won by a hundred yards, the amateur bringing his boat up half full of water to the shore, where the amphibians stood with long faces.

'She's water-logged, she's half full; no boat can sail like that,' said the amateur, getting out; and the seared old faces brightened, for here was a real excuse. So they all agreed in chorus: 'Nothing could be done with a water-logged boat,' and the oldest amphibian, who had been the loudest in his abuse and criticism, said condescendingly—

'I think you've done remarkably well.'

The amateur held his peace.

The Young Rover was sunk beneath the blue waves of the lagoon in order that she might stanch, and the race postponed for two days.

The night before the second trial the amateur sat with a group of gunners, marshmen, and wherrymen listening to an animated conversation, from which the words 'rocking keels,' 'straight bows,' 'lug-sails' and 'cutter-sails,' 'litha masts,' and so on, flashed forth. It was wonderful the excitement and interest shown about boats. Then they turned to the amateur and began to praise his work, but he was unmoved.

Next morning the vanes showed the wind blew from the nor'-east, a nice, fresh breeze, as *The Young Rover* was hoisted from the hard bottom of the lagoon and dressed with her sail. At half-past eleven the amateur took his seat in *The Young Rover* and the old broadsman took his seat at the tiller of *The Little Maid,* and away they went to the starting-stake, sailing up dead-level, and at the word slacking out the sheets and going off before the wind like two greyhounds.

The amateur soon shot ahead and raced past *The Little Maid*, luffing round the stake first, but immediately he got on the wind *The Little Maid* began to pick-up, and before the second stake was reached the old broadsman had shot past *The Young Rover*

Then the amphibians on the bank began to swear and criticise and mob the amateur, for *The Young Rover* could neither turn nor handle, and this was all attributed to the amateur's bad watermanship.

As they tacked up to the starting-stake and luffed round it the umpire registered the times—

(1) *The Little Maid*: time, 37 minutes.

(2) *The Young Rover*: time, 39 minutes.

And away they went for the second round of three miles, running down to the first stake, leading to the second stake, and leading back to the first stake and round it, tacking to the starting-place, and so finishing the second round thus :—

(1) *The Little Maid*: time, 39 minutes

(2) *The Young Rover*: time, 43½ minutes.

The broadsman sailed in to the starter smiling with triumph ; the amateur sailed in looking grim but collected

After throwing two bags of ballast out of *The Little Maid*, and moving the two remaining sand-bags, the amateur took his seat in his own boat and the broadsman took *The Young Rover*.

'Now you'll see *The Young Rover* trosh to windward like a racehorse Now we shall see what she'll do, when she's properly handled,' said the irate natives   Away the boats staited amid much excitement, *The Young Rover* leading to the first stake; but directly the first stake was passed the amateur in *The Little Maid* shot up to windward and went sailing past *The Young Rover,* and as the natives watched *The Little Maid* showing a clean pair of heels, they marvelled open-mouthed.

Away went *The Little Maid's* skipper down and up the lagoon, luffing round the stake and handling his little boat like a thing of life; and the umpire recorded the fiist round—

(1) *The Little Maid*: time, 40 minutes

(2) *The Young Rover*: time, 42 minutes.

'Our boat will pick him up the second round,' they said, as the boats ran down before the wind; but the amateur only increased his lead, and came in a winner by five minutes, the times of the second round being—

(1) *The Little Maid*: 36 minutes.   .

(2) *The Young Rover*: 41 minutes

And as the boats sailed up to the staith the old broadsman in *The Young Rover* looked crestfallen, and remarked he was never so sucked in in all his life   The owner of *The Young Rover* blushed purple; and several of the critics who had been abusing the amateur came up and told him they had mobbed him, that they couldn't believe their eyes when he won, and that he had sailed as well as the old broadsman   And the old broadsman tuined and said—

'Yes, he is nigh as good as me.   I told you so.'

'Well, well,' said an old amphibian, who had been loudest

in his abuse of the amateur, 'I'll never speak about a man sailing a boat no more, unless I see whether his boat be right first. There was I laying it on to the awkwardness of the gentleman, and arter all he hev done the quickest round in both boats.'

But one old fellow in the corner stood muttering that he didn't believe the little warmin of a jolly could beat their boat, and he'd sail the old broadsman.

The amateur offered a money prize, and away they started, the unconvinced broadsman in *The Young Rover*, and the amateur's rival in *The Little Maid*. *The Little Maid* passed *The Young Rover* before the first stake in running before the wind, and the old amphibian was so surely beaten at the end of the first round that he gave in with curses. The times were—

The Little Maid: 37 minutes.

The Young Rover: 44 minutes

And after all, the much-abused amateur had sailed the quickest rounds of any—

In *The Little Maid* in 36 minutes.

In *The Young Rover* in 39 minutes

But the amateur's reputation, as well as that of his boat, was securely established from that day on the broad, and the amphibians discovered that, after all, he had learnt from a '*native*,' and 'as he often lay on the lagoon, he was just like one of themselves.'

And the amateur, as he sat in his saloon at dinner, felt the seat rising and falling, and the sides of the cabin seemed to be slipping and sliding and all the world to be falling, as one sees it after coming off a very stormy passage at sea; and one can only wonder whether birds see our world with a rolling vision when they alight, so greatly are our senses affected by a fifteen-mile sail.

XII

FIRST VOICE OF SPRING

HE wild wastes of yellow reed and blue water that gleamed from afar beneath yesterday's garish sunshine and cold easterly breath, that spun the mill-sails round like children's pin-wheels, and filled the big black sails of the wherries, were now more sober in colour,—the yellow had turned to a delicate amber, the waters were silvery grey, a soft curtain of mist hung over the distant moorlands, whence the voice of a mavish floated dreamily in the heavy air.

Yesterday the sky was azure, not a cloud as large as an iris-bloom was to be seen; but to-day the sky was full of light and graceful forms, shallop-like clouds that floated with fantastic sails lazily through the silvery dome.

It was the first day of spring; and as I looked over the calm, soft grey wastes, I heard in the still, moist air a faint croak, like the creaking of a leathery hinge. With lips apart I listened again to catch the welcome sound, and ere long from a shiny dike-way I heard a short sleepy croak. The frogs hopped from the warm holes underneath the clumps of old rush and reed, and slid lazily into the warming waters, for the sun rose higher each day in his course, and spread a subtle influence over amphibians, and birds, and beasts.

Towards the afternoon a soft sunshine lit up the moist landscape, and made the wondrous harmonies of amber and silver glow and swell. The distant windmills rose from the misty marshland like tall sea-lanterns guarding the sluggish land from the yellow sandhills, that rolled on to the marsh like breakers of the roaring sea, whose plaintive voice sang its soft crooning dirge upon the wet sea-beaches beyond.

Under the warming influence of the white light the voice of the slimy, black-stained frogs became more frequent and bolder, and ere nightfall the dikes resounded with their strange song, sung down in the bowels of the earth.

As the spring sun settled red behind the reed-tossed fretted sky, and left the marshland to darkness and to me, there flashed before my mind the delicate glowing landscape of amber and silver-grey, through which the soft croaking voice of spring resounded, filling the senses with a lasting music, as the music of the sea lurks ever in the beautiful spotted shells gathered from dead coral beaches.

XIII

A HORSE-DEALER'S DEATH—LAST WISH

THE old horse-dealer lay dying in his little marsh farm, where he still kept some good-looking screws and fattened some measly Irish cattle. The solicitor had been called in hastily to make his will, and when he offered the old man a stylographic pen wherewith to sign his name, the invalid looked up with a humorous smile, and said—

'Do that write cedar or ink, bor?'

'Ink,' replied the commonplace young lawyer.

'Ay,' said the old dealer, tracing his name in shaky characters over the blue paper; then dropping the black pen with its bright brass band, he said calmly—

'Death-watches—I hear 'em ticking!'

And the solicitor and witness—the old man's steward—withdrew, his only son entering.

'Boy, I'm going soon; one big jump over the brook and I shall be gone. Look here, lad, when we've jumped, lay me under the straw and muck in the bullock-yard; that will do me fine. I don't want no parsons nor funerals about here.

and all that long-faced, solemn-looking lot, black as a wet Friday. Promise, lad ! '

'I promise, father.'

And the old horse-dealer settled down in his bed, and died with a humorous smile on his brave and wasted features

XIV

A STUDY IN GOLD AND BLUE

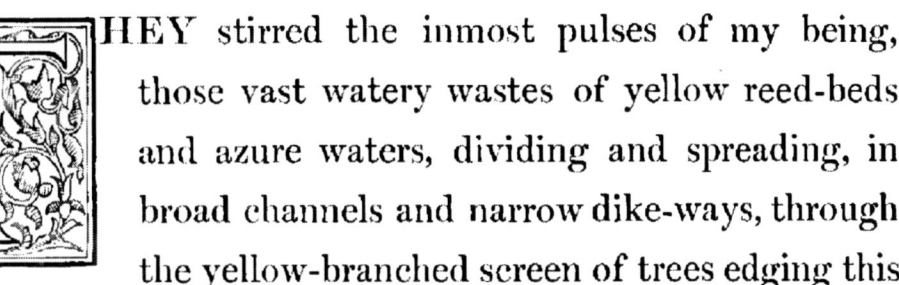HEY stirred the inmost pulses of my being, those vast watery wastes of yellow reed-beds and azure waters, dividing and spreading, in broad channels and narrow dike-ways, through the yellow-branched screen of trees edging this strange, wild land, and beating, in each drop of their blue circulations, with the great tidal pulse of life—the never-ceasing ebb and flow—a subtle influence that swells the water under the bridges by the mills, where the swallows fashion their warmly lined nests from the ooze that caresses the distant stalks of the farthest reed-beds, that glow in the bright sun and are waved by the cold wind that steals over the crests of the marram-knit dunes.

Outside these shifting sand-dunes, where the gay swallows hunt for flies in the summer afternoons, the same influence is working, rolling in the great breakers that beat upon the shifting beaches, battling into thin spray, and rushing up the smooth sands with a sharp, sweeping hiss; then they yellow the atmosphere as the broken, frothy water rushes back to the

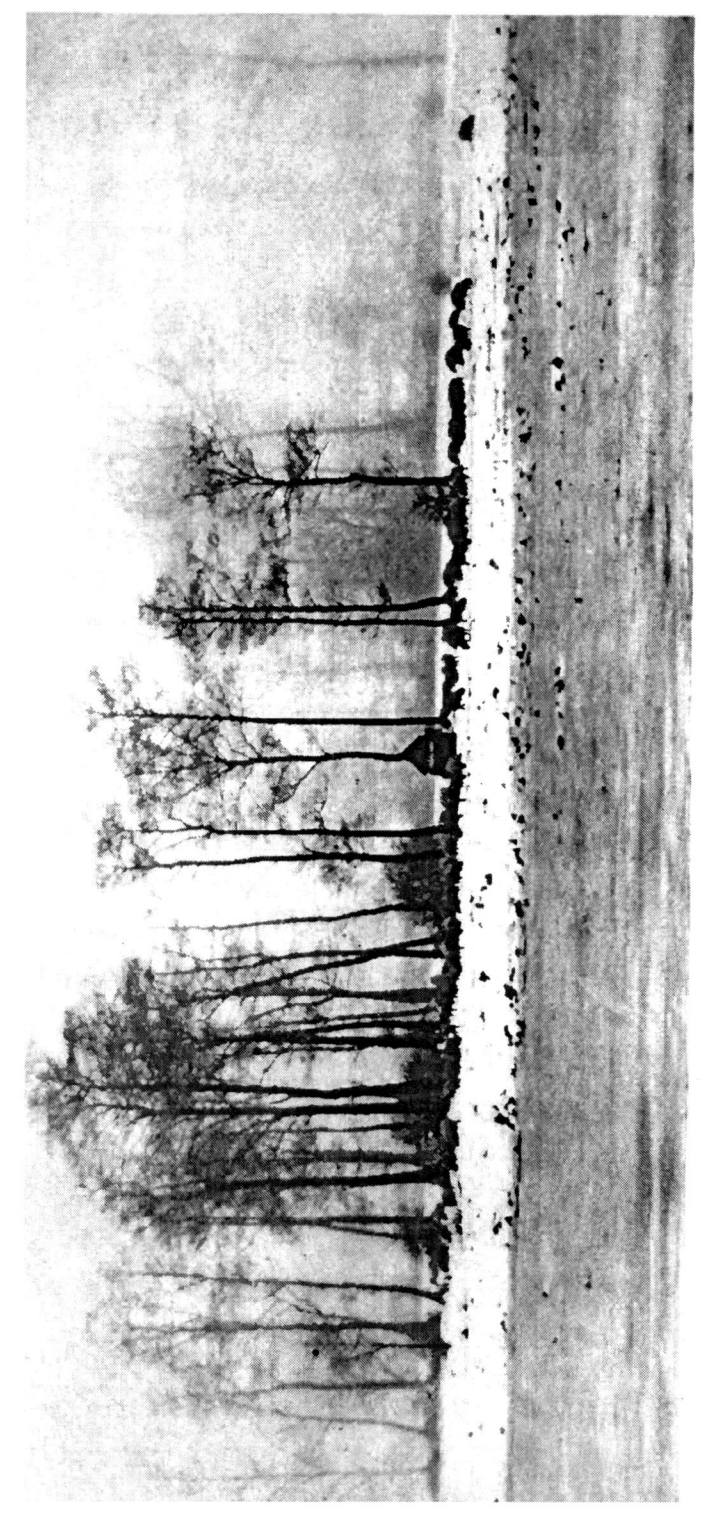

a wild music—a manly, musical song of war and wrestling, whether in the embrace of a mistress or the grip of the foe.

And only the desolate, wind-sculptured hollows of the dunes keep the blue waters from mixing, and gaining the mastery of the sopping land, where the flocks feed, and the watery tribe of birds cradle their young.

But as we gaze over the golden and azure land, and watch the quickly circling mill-sails and gliding ships, and then stand and listen to the roar of the sea beyond the sandhills, and as we watch the stealthy blue tide creep softly, like a serpent, up the rushy ooze of the shores, one cannot but rejoice in one's manhood, and in the brave hearts gone to rest before us. Big and loyal hearts gone down with the mighty Vikings who quailed not before man or beast, nor before the titanic forces of nature, but fought and conquered from the roaring sea a beautiful land all gold and blue, where they might fight and work, eat and drink and love, and live a brave life that should not make the spirits of their forefathers weep when they turned their sad eyes from the limitless night upon their sons—the men of the land of Gold and Blue.

XV

COUNTRY COCKNEYS

NE grey November day a little marsh farmer, his friend, and two hobble-de-hoys—natives of the neighbouring parish, where they had lived all their days scaring birds, and tending bullocks, and leading the drill-horse—started off to do a little pheasant shooting in a carr which the two friends had stocked with birds, drawn from the squire's neighbouring coverts, by using currants, raisins, and maize sown broadcast as lures; for pheasants are wayward, and given to wandering afar, whereas the homely partridge will never go far from the place wherein he was bred.

The farmer, who was a deadly shot, posted himself where he could stop the birds, whilst his friend followed the two lads who acted as beaters.

The two guns were on the tiptoe of expectation, every nerve on the strain, as they stood with lips open, the better to hear the first rustle caused by their quarry.

The country lads liked the new work, and beat vigorously at first; but suddenly they seemed to be occupied in studying a clump of bramble bearing unripe fruit, for the season had been cold and wet.

The guns stood silent as statues, when through the clear, chill air they heard the elder lad say—

'What be these?'

To which the younger beater replied—

'You fule, don't you know?'

'No'

'They be blackberries, then,' retorted the junior.

'I never knew berries were red when they're black.'

'Consarned you for a fule! they're allust red when they're green,' said the younger boy.

And there were two explosions of laughter from the sportsmen

XVI

BIRD'S SLEEP

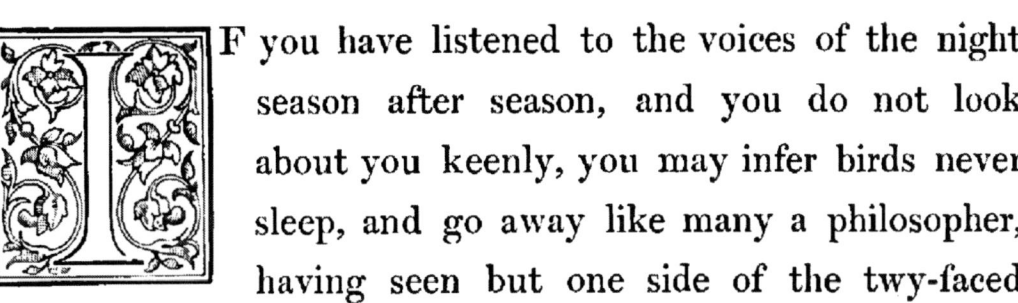F you have listened to the voices of the night season after season, and you do not look about you keenly, you may infer birds never sleep, and go away like many a philosopher, having seen but one side of the twy-faced shield. For birds do sleep. Need I tell you that the lark sleeps in a grassy form on the marsh bottom, as you shall know by her dung. The wagtails and peewits, too, sleep on the marshes, whilst the little 'blackcaps' roost where the rats forage in the sedge and rush, dreaming perhaps of the harriers that roost on the wall, or heaps of poled litter that dot the marshland, or on the dry 'hills,' as the slightest elevations in the marshland are called, for all things go by comparison.

Every hedgerow, too, is filled with sleeping finches; most empty holes in trees have their living tenants, either wren or tit, and the lower branches of trees afford minstrel thrushes a cosy bed, whilst the reed-beds are warm dormitories for reed-warbler and reed-pheasant, for rail, coot and water-hen and on the open water is a soft bed for fowl and swans, that you may see with their heads curled over their soft backs, floating like ships anchored upon an idle mere. All things must sleep, as all things must die, and these are the two sureties of life.

XVII

VISIONS

 LAY sleeping in my yacht, and as I slept I dreamt this dream :—

The world was a series of rivers, intersecting low hills spread out on a flat earth far as eye could reach. I dreamt I was living in a phantom ship, and was not of the world. My ship seemed for ever to be sailing on the grey waterways, and the sun shone and the red-brick houses were reddened across the grey marshes, and my ship was everlastingly wafted over the great waters.

My ears were filled with delight as I looked upon the birds and flocks and yellow water-plants, and I was filled with peace; yet whenever my phantom ship drew near those fairy towns on the low hills, my heart quickened, and I would steer the ship to go up amongst the red houses, and land and look about dark corners and into dark doorways and up desolate streets, for I was seeking the faces of women, for they all seemed more beautiful in those red houses than when I saw them working upon the marshland; that seemed to make them hard and angular. But the soft light under the roofs seemed to round off their figures and fill their faces with understanding, and in those visits I would meet strange, and often stranger-spoken, men and women and children, dressed in fantastic and grotesque colours that offended me, for I had only known the delicate silver-grey of the heron's back, and the delicate orpiment of the iris, and the pale blue of the skies, and these coarse colours hurt me, as a rough surface passed over the face hurts it. But these people brought forth strange fluids in bottles, and some were sweet and good, and they had dainty ways of preparing food that I knew not of; but they were so sluggish and lazy that I noticed they did not enjoy these things as they might have done, and their fat and shapeless bodies told me they ate too much

When my senses were lulled by the sweet and pleasant drinks and foods, I to some extent forgot the terrible oppression and blows their crude-coloured and shapeless clothes had given me. I thought in my surfeit that to lead such a life might be pleasant; but I was soon undeceived, for as soon as they had shut their mouths from eating they opened them to bite their neighbours, and all manner of lies and calumnies crawled out, as out of a foul pit; and they instructed me, and I learned how they were always fighting in a stealthy, womanish way with their tongues, and the black arts of vanity and calumny, for I too liked fighting, but as a man

But I saw when I revisited some of the largest of that cluster of houses that the men concealed themselves in the same kind of dresses so that they might the better fight their stealthy fight, and they came not armed as a knight, with a blazoned shield, but like a gliding snake, all of one colour And I watched and saw how men rotted in their cities, as they called these houses, and how they were soft-hearted, and could not bear pain nor fatigue, but ran about like roaring wolves, greedily devouring in the moment women as they did pears—for all things to them were labelled to be eaten or not, and most cared only for things to be eaten. And they spent their days in backbiting, and robbing, and struggling to gather up heaps of gold to buy more luscious things, for they dwelt not on the virtue of the thing, but, like ravening animals, tore greedily their food, and adjudged it rich and rare by the number of gold pieces it cost

Then I found there were some wiser, who sought none of these things, but they were thin and hungry-looking, like a starved snipe when the wind and frost bind the water-brooks; but I heard they were accursed with the gift of pale thought, that sicklied o'er their lives, and they told me that these pursued a painted moth called Vanity; for in that strange world some were proud that they should know more than their fellows.

And I would have learned other things, how the people of these houses thought themselves so superior to the people of the marshes, but they were not; and it is said that one day the men of the marshes intended to arise and burn all the red houses, and take the beautiful women therein and breed up a new race, beautiful and strong, brave and hard, growing like the oaks

But the men of the houses brag, for they are like unto women in all things, that they have made a thing they call civilisation, and they set great store thereby; but I found that the more the people lived in the house-clusters the more monstrous and feeble were they, and as I sailed on, in my dream, I found that those were happiest and best who chose to live in the fields, for such became men even though they had been as women in the houses.

But I too was becoming womanish in the town, and very quickly, for I had begun to talk of dress, and to love to see what every dirty worm who wriggled more than his neighbour did, and I loved strong drink, and could not eat like a man; and just as my disease broke out, I was snatched back to my ship, and became whole.

And I suddenly awoke, to find myself rolling backwards and forwards in my boat, for my yacht was beating to windward across a tidal water; and as I looked round, my lips involuntarily shaped themselves, and I heard myself mutter—

'Our civilisation is a grotesque failure'; and sweet lips in the saloon said gently—

'Not whilst there is some one to love !'

And I replied, 'No,' and 'Yes,' 'Yes,' and 'No.'

For such is the only answer to any problem, but this waspish, womanish age requires a positive 'Yea' or 'Nay.'

XVIII

CUCKOO-TIME

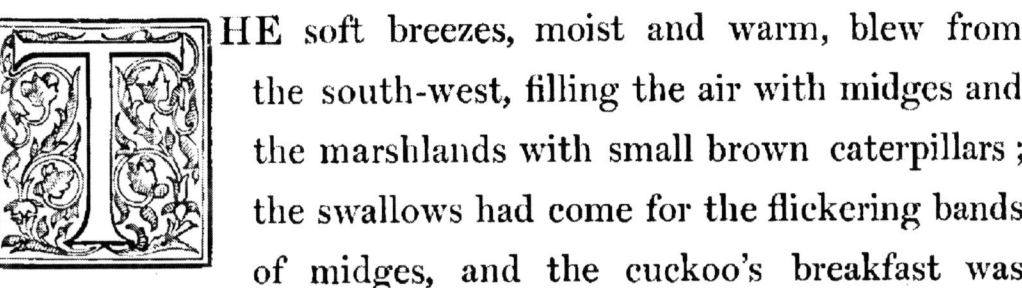HE soft breezes, moist and warm, blew from the south-west, filling the air with midges and the marshlands with small brown caterpillars; the swallows had come for the flickering bands of midges, and the cuckoo's breakfast was awaiting him all unconsciously, for his early food is the brown caterpillar, occasionally varied by a dish of fine, fresh mavis's eggs.

The sun shone brightly, and the fenland, now growing tinged with green, stretched far away to a distant coppice, all blue in the morning sunshine, when suddenly the first welcome sound echoed through the still, soft landscape, the six clear notes of the blue cuckoo breathed from the sleeping, blue distance, immediately calling to mind the Welsh and English saying, that the cuckoo's voice is not clear until he shall have sucked a number of blue mavis's eggs. The Saxon peasant believes too that his years are numbered even as the number of the cuckoo's notes first heard by him in the springtide.

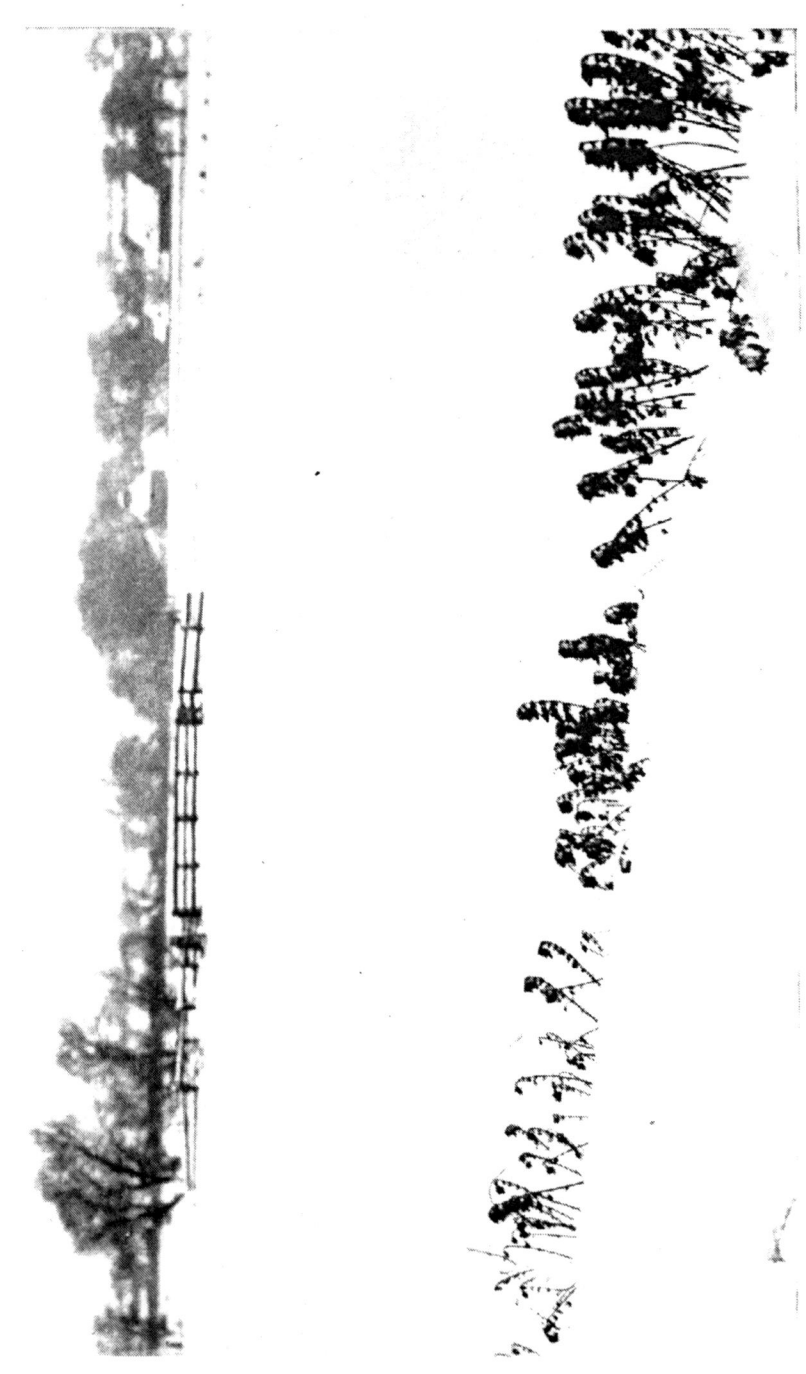

As I listened, again the vibrating echo of his voice sounded in the blue misty trees; and when the last notes had melted away in the soft music of the breezes, one realised how this strange bird-voice spake the sentiment of the mysterious blue mists.

XIX

FINE LADIES

THEY were fine, well-formed, fresh, good-looking village maidens, and they were being educated to be *ladies*. Their hard-working father had risen in the world, for his heart, like that of all true men, was in his work. Indeed, his work was his second self, and in this case his dearest self, for his aspirations were neither self-seeking nor spiritual.

Next to his work he loved his wife, as all good men do. He would have reversed the order in which I placed the objects of his affections,—so would most true men,—but a man's heart is hidden to himself.

His wife was a joyous, sensuous woman, all pulse and dash. She loved soft and gay raiment, was naturally refined and possessed of good taste, for to drop an aspirate, or eat peas with her knife, was impossible to this splendidly moulded woman, with hair like bulrush down, and an eye the colour of speedwell. Moreover, she was faithful, and his daughters were his own—his very own. This splendid woman was faithful, because she realised—for she had brains — how her tame and rather methodical husband spent never a farthing on himself, and gave her all his increasing income to lavish on herself and daughters, whilst he went about his tasks in old clothes, like unto those worn in the days of his early struggles; for habit is the strongest of masters.

Moreover, this joyous queen was grateful to him in her way; she never murmured at the dull life led by her in the commonplace little town, but ate, and drank, and dressed richly, and tossed the money about freely, even unto waste. And yet the poor round about prospered: this prodigality blew cold joints and stale bread in plenty to the neighbouring cottages.

As her children grew up, this darling of the sun, whose fine, smooth features began to mark with crows' feet, spent her time in educating them, for she was determined they should be ladies, though, good soul, she had no more idea what the word meant than the raw Scotsman knows the meaning of *wit*—wut, he would say.

They were taught to play the piano, and they confused coarse emotions with music, and preferred Offenbach to Beethoven, and 'The Song of the Hall,' to 'The Twa Corbies.' They, too, dressed brightly, neither crudely, primitively, nor in sham aesthetic gowns; but they could not attain the perfect tonist in dress, for such an one requires to be born an artist. One would wear a light blue ribbon with brown tailor-made coat, and say it was refined; but a different shade of brown upon brown was a mystery as hidden to them as the cipher on the stone of Rosetta. Their jewellery was commonplace in manufacture, but not vulgar either in carat or quantity. The big mother had too good taste to lend herself unto such trinkets, for instinctively she felt that a gleaming jewel to complete the *ensemble* of the costume must be used as carefully as a note of colour in a decorative scheme Indeed, your most artistic people never wear jewellery for its own sake, save when dressed for the evening Your greatest artist wears no blazing diamonds upon his fingers, but leaves that to coarse beer-sellers and prosperous traders Suffice it to say, none of them possessed a string of pearls, those perfect jewels when encircling a lovely woman's throat.

When the large-hearted mother had taught them what she knew that was 'genteel,' they were forbidden to sew or to go into the kitchen under any pretext, they were sent to school to learn a string of doubtful stories called history; they were taught geography—four pages a day,—grammar (Lindley Murray), and other vain matters, and in the fulness of time the proud mother looked upon five jolly, fresh, brightly dressed 'ladies,' who were so educated that they could not sew a button to their gloves, and knew not how to make a cup of tea or boil an egg. But most of all they did not know the value of money; the father always gave them plenty

But alas for the methods of the middle-class! no gentleman mistook them for ladies; they could not understand those men who were very jolly, and kind, and humorous, but never offered marriage

One day, one—the eldest—who was really very friendly

with an accomplished gentleman, artfully turned the conversation on education, and in a subtle way asked how girls should best be trained to become ladies, for she affected an interest in educational matters.

'There is but *one* way,' he said, 'and that's quite simple, but it's the only way. The pupil must be born and bred amongst ladies and gentlemen.'

'But that's impossible for so many,' said the girl calmly. 'What is the best training for them?'

'To be able to sew, cook, and keep house,' he answered; and turning to her sister he asked, 'Don't you think so, Annie?'

'Ye-e-s,' she faltered.

'Can you sew and cook, Annie?' he asked tenderly, taking her lovely hand; for her fingers tapered, though she was of the plebs.

'No-o-o,' she faltered, ashamed for once of her accomplishments.

'Well, Annie, I love you, darling, and if you will have me I'll marry you, but you must learn to sew and cook first.'

For he too had theories in this experimental age; he wanted a strong, fresh wife, for, as he said—

'To renovate the stock you must go to the soil.'

XX

GROWING WEATHER

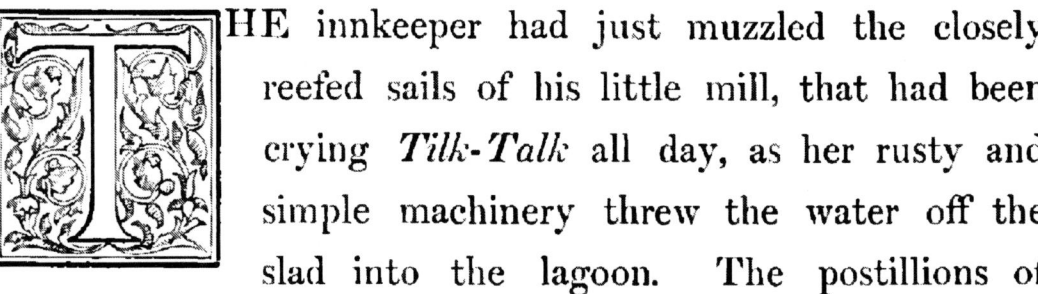HE innkeeper had just muzzled the closely reefed sails of his little mill, that had been crying *Tilk-Talk* all day, as her rusty and simple machinery threw the water off the slad into the lagoon. The postillions of the storm—some big, gleaming drops of water—sent him hurriedly to his home amongst the elms, as they galloped past him and brought up with patterings upon my window-pane.

Closely fastening the transparent glass so that I could, with difficulty, see the tethered mill-sails tugging doggedly at the mooring-rope, which was, however, a stout bit of hemp, I sat in a delightfully artificial, exotic atmosphere, for the little tortoise-stove, with her red mouth open two inches wide, burned with a smothered rage on my right, whilst the storm shrieked and blew in through the inch of window left open to windward. The atmosphere within the boat being a delightfully impartial and tranquil one, the curtain blew idly about the saloon; the rings rattled, and blocks and ropes on the mast played drum-taps to the merry piping of the wind.

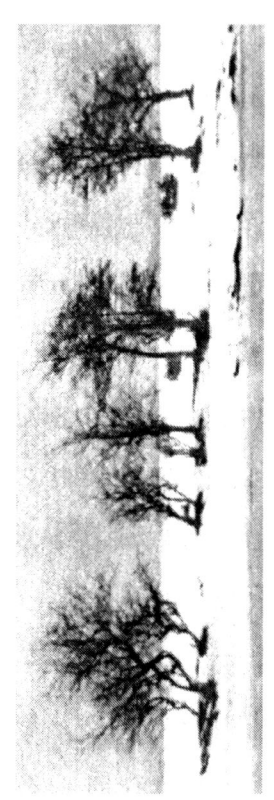

The marshman had said in the morning that this was 'growing weather,' the constituents of which are a warm temperature, rain, and blowy weather, so an oracular old person, wearing a moleskin cap, and complaining of lumbago, informed me. Yes, he persisted that he had seen turnips and mangolds grow as much (he did not say whether in girth or height) in one day in such weather as they did in a week of mild, ungrowing weather.

'The wind work 'em about, that make 'em grow,' he said, with a knowing wink.

And it is true. I have seen vegetation move, as you may see the short hand of a clock move, after the southerly or south-westerly gale in early spring. But the old man did not know that was a fecundating wind, as the pale flowers of grasses, trees, and other wind-fertilised plants know.

Moreover, the wind had blown the water across the lagoon, and the water in my narrow mooring bay struck there wider and higher than it did at sunrise. The fury of the squalls at times shook my table, and brought curious and adventurous drops of rain to my paper, but still a fulfar on a marsh holl began to sing its love-song; the unceasing fury of the storm, however, stopped the beatings of its speckled throat, for the wind is like his brother musicians, filled with jealousy. He was determined no music but his own pipings and drummings, his own wave-lappings and wind-cracklings, should be heard; and yet once or twice the gay storm-cock again and again essayed to add his wild notes to the storm, for a brave heart, though enslaved, is never killed.

XXI

DROPPED EGGS

S you wander over the green marshland in early spring, when the dikes are sprinkled with the water-crowsfoot, and the beautiful yellow wagtails cleave the air like living flames, you may find dropped eggs—eggs unnested, unattended, uncared for—little pledges of love, dropped secretly, or in haste, in some lonely corner. You may find the eggs of nearly every ordinary bird dropped in this mysterious manner, an you make these foundlings the subject of statistical inquiries, as do curious men. You will find the most immoral of birds are the mavises, blackbirds, storm-cocks, robins, hedge-sparrows, house-sparrows (I can believe anything of them), reed buntings, yellow wagtails, sedge-warblers, reed-warblers, starlings and larks, and you will, by the same standard of life, find the snipe and cuckoo the most moral of birds,—they never drop any eggs carelessly in sly corners.

XXII

GOLD AND BRONZE

LL day we had sailed through a bright, cold landscape, for the wind had blown across the eastern sandhills from rosy morn, almost without change; though there were stray puffs from other points of the horizon, puffs that made our scarlet vane hesitate and turn from the orient, and at the same time made the great white sail flop. These wandering breaths were inconstant and short-blown, and soon the tin lady with the great bunch of flowers was indicating the east, and the sail was full and drawing on our sheet, making the boat heel over and bubble over the tideway.

And when the yellow sun began to bulge behind the trees, a flood of yellow light bathed the marshland, streaming on the bronze-gold crops of the flat-land. Then was the world transfigured. The blue rims of fairy-like trees yellowed, the mills gilded with refined gold, the golden mill-sails, tinged with silvery grey, fluttered like the wings of some fantastic bird. Even the bronze marsh-gates were bathed in an ethereal golden vapour, and the land was a harmony in gold and bronze, a metallic *chef-d'œuvre* of the east wind.

XXIII

CONSCIENCE MUCK-RAKE

MANY years ago Farmer Mason was a prosperous flockmaster, and Jesse Jakes was a shrewd amateur horse-dealer and poacher. But a broken river-wall, floods and fluke, ruined the flockmaster, and he left Hasemere. On the other hand, Jakes saved money enough to take a little farm, and he became a respectable church-goer, voting always for the Tories.

One little matter weighed on his conscience: he had stolen a muck-rake from Farmer Mason in the old days. Years after, Farmer Mason, after a hard battle, returned to Hasemere and took a small farm next to Jakes's land, the two farmers' houses facing each other. Upon old Michaelmas Day the farmer moved in, and Jakes was very neighbourly, lending a hand in unpacking the van, and helping all he could. And every day he asked Farmer Mason if he didn't want a muck-rake.

At last the farmer had need of the tool, and Jakes hurried off with a delighted face and brought back Farmer Mason's old muck-rake, telling him he was welcome to it. And Jakes was a happier man ever afterwards.

XXIV

A NIGHT WALK IN EARLY SPRING

PRIL 4th. Spring had come in dry and bright, and the sere marshes and green reeds looked thirsty in the setting sun, as they stood like sentinels along the river-banks, looking out for the first swallows, which had that evening flown in from the sea, and hawked low for the midges circling about the reed-stalks.

.   .   .   .   .

It was midnight as I passed through the wood, already turning green under the hot, bright day, but never a sound could I hear. No animal called; not a cock-pheasant moved restlessly; no sitting wild-duck left the carr; the very silence of the moonlit night filled one's senses with a primeval thrill of alertness, such as must have filled the hearts of our ancestors when some savage beast rushed from its lair in the peaceful wood; but nothing could I hear till I left the wood, and walked along the marsh-wall towards the mist-masked river. As I walked along beneath the dim light the dikes gleamed and resounded with frogs disturbed in their nocturnal love embraces. So quick were they that the silent, dusky waters were dimpled in countless places, and lo! the slimy creatures were gone to the weedy depths. As I walked on, the bare willows seemed to sleep peacefully and brightly, and one walked by softly, as if afraid to waken them. They took on human attributes in the misty moonlight, their hard contours and feathery crowns softened into an ethereal effeminacy that charmed. Away across the marsh a white cloud of mist lay heavy, and reached up half-mast on the wherries, gliding noiselessly along the silent waterway.

. . . As I stepped from the quaking bog to my boat, a speckled owl flew *heavily*—so fairy-like and stilly was the misty night,—shrieking over the reed-tops.

XXV

A SAD DOCUMENT

SHE was a fair rose, as fair, refined, and distinguished as the gay pink anemone blooms, frilled with white petals, that stood on a table beside her.

We were sitting on a sofa talking when she arose and, going to a drawer, took thence a coarsely printed red-bound pamphlet, upon which a rudely engraved bee-hive stood surrounded by crudely cut flowers.

'Why,' she asked, 'does this pamphlet always make me sad when I look upon it?'

I took it, turned the thing about and about, and discovered that it was the prize-list of the *St. Joseph Cottage Garden Society* for the previous year. As I looked into it, I too-felt the sordidness of the thing: the lists of patrons, committees, judges, and prize-winners—obscure persons of undoubted respectability—speaking the *vanitas vanitatum.* As I pondered on these names I could imagine the heart-burnings many must have had when a second-rate country surgeon's wife was made Lady President, or when an upstart landlord was made Vice-President, or when the Rev. Archer Burne-

Smith's wife was put upon the Ladies' Committee. Then when I came upon the name of an impudent busybody who, though a surgeon, called himself Dr. Jones, sprinkled over half a dozen pages of print, I knew why the organ of this inoffensive and well-intentioned Cottage Gardener's Society was so offensive: it was the petty Debrett of a petty parish —the parish book of snobs. And since my high-born lady friend despised the legends of the real Debrett, it was no matter for wonder that the petty wrigglings of the village worms should sadden her noble soul.

This much I told her, and her smiles returned as she said simply—

'Beautiful souls have no Debrett; everybody is equal before the Goddess of Love.'

XXVI

A LANDSCAPE

I WAS lying in some warm bents on a salting, and breathing the warm air of the spring-tide, looking up into the boundless fading azure, my burning cheeks fanned by the tonic dry and cool east wind that blew up the tideway, raising the greenish waters into frothy waves, and ruffling the feathers of the flocks of widgeon that flashed in waves upon the shallows, the watchman whistling his soft 'All's well' as they fed upon the marine grasses, or preened their feathers, or watched the great gulls feeding on the mud-worms. For the tide was ebbing, leaving great tracts of wrack-strown slub, stretching on either side of the bleached and green posts, beacons of the channel to the fairy, red-tiled old fishing-town, lifted in the heated air high out of the green, and flashing above the tide like a misty, red-petalled flower, and all the air was filled with the savour and odours of salt wrack. And the landscape seemed to be a dream, for the white-hot sun made all the scene burn, and palpitate, and flash, and whirl round and round, as do the dust particles in a shimmering beam of light, and the wild cries of the

gulls transported one to a fairy world where all was topsy-turvy, for a mirage was on the flats, and one was whirled away into a palpitating world, where all things were lovely and impalpable, yet full of delicious colour, and life, and motion—a magic world where dwelt the joyous spirits of all earthly things—spiritual worlds, flats, cities, and lands— the pale and sweet-coloured souls of things that had been. . . . And such are sweet memories.

XXVII

THE TWO WAYS

E were sailing before a stiff breeze when I grew drowsy and lay down on the berth. The soft rocking of the ship as I rolled gently from one side to the other, the pleasant creaking of the bulkhead, and the wash of the waves outside, all lulled me into a delightful sleep that I shall never forget, for the last thing remembered by me was that I was being borne through space on the wings of the wind. And then I dreamt I saw a lovely woman clad in delicate orpiment, with a purple crown of flowers round her dark locks; in her right hand she carried a scarlet poppy, and in her left was a spray reft from a birch-tree. She seemed to float before my eyes, her yellow garb burning with a deeper, redder glow, and she held her hands towards me and said—

'My son, choose.'

And I dreamt she added—

'The poppy is the emblem of success, and the possessor shall be bright and distinguished before the eyes of men; but he who chooses the poppy must first press the juice from the stem and drink, for his soul must be fettered in sleep or ever the charm worketh But to him that holdeth the birchen emblem there is no fame, and his path shall be hard, even unto death, for he must live ever for his ideal, and not in glorious riches, as the possessors of the poppy, and he has no reward; and if he be not reviled of men, yet shall he get no fame, nor shall his name be in men's mouths, but he shall have ever a green strength, for the virtue will never depart from the birchen twig, and that shall be his only reward, that he may live for his ideal.

'Now choose, my son,' said the beautiful lady with the shining face, and she held both hands towards me; and I heard myself make answer in a far-off voice—

'Sweet lady, when I was yet a child, a fair lady wove a birchen wreath for me, and she placed it with her own dainty hands upon my head, so I had no choice.'

And the lady smiled a sweet smile.

'But your choice, what is your choice, my son?'

And I felt troubled in my sleep, and said—

'Sweet lady, the white milk of the poppy is sweet, but the green sap of the birch is sweeter.'

And I felt the white arms of the fair woman around me, and she pressed me to her glowing bosom, where I forgot all things until I was awakened by a crashing noise The sail had jibed.

XXVIII

RETURN OF SPRING

ARCH, the month of cold winds and hail-storms and wind-frosts, was half spent. April, the moon of cold, hard, easterly winds, alternating with south-westerly skies, of rime-frosts and sparkling sheet-ice, was nearing.

For many a day the hard blue sky, covering the colour-less reedy landscape and pale sere marshes, had glared over-head, making the waters look hard and blue and clear, and silencing the love-songs of the birds, making them shrink and huddle together in the withered tatters of last summer's lush crops.

But last night the yellow moon made the rime-powder sparkle on the dried plant-skeletons of the flats, and this morning flakes of fairy ice, in fairy pictures, grew from my window-panes. I could feel before I arose that a south-westerly wind was blowing. My skin was no longer dry and smooth like the reed-stalks, but swollen out and modelled; the light and shade played in and out of the little hollows

to flow wildly and healthily through my body, just as the sap was rising in the young plants on the marshland.

As I dressed, I could hear from my window the voices of the birds over the marshland ; larks were carolling, and over there by the grey-green willow-carrs snipe laughed, and away by that tossing reedy bed, crooning plaintively, were the frogs in the dikes, who croaked and crooned their soft love-songs, so long silent. But when I peeped forth into the fairy scene my heart leapt within me In the river before me the water was richer and softer in colour ; it looked like a living fluid now, where fish might spawn, and not like unto the icy cold mixture of gases, seen in the frail alembics of the laboratory.

But all round my horizon the landscape gleamed with living colour ; the poor shrunken landscape of yesterday, with its hard details, was now a fairy scene under the magic touches of the dew and mist, and caressing south-westerly wind.

Far away over the water, reeds that now appeared to grow in picturesque clumps peeped with dark tassels over the delicately blue trees in the uplands, forming a harmony indescribable, a delicacy of colour inimitable.

And now the greenish-blue clumps of marshland had grown more impressive and beautiful , the hard little coppice of yesterday was now a gorgeous fairy wood rising into the ambient air, and soft fleecy clouds floated across the pale, vapouring, grey-blue sky.

And as one looked over the noble harmonious scene spreading beyond, to the foot of the land, the eye would settle for a moment, here and there, on an exquisite little picture, some marsh farm, seen behind a decorative fringe of reed tassel, palpitating in its blue envelope of transfiguring mist.

Then, turning away towards the softly sounding sea, the sandhills showed a wan white above the green fields of the marshland, and through all and over all the sweet-voiced birds sang. Even the sluggish rivers and waterways meandered with the mysterious pulse of life, and at our feet the pulse beat of life through the world, for warm and living spring had escaped from the chill grip of the wintry east wind. And one could not forget that it was on this day many years ago that a brave man died that the world might be filled with love; nor did he perish in vain, as the peaceful landscape with its magic beauty and safe retreats has proved, for by love, fellowship, and bravery alone were these waters reclaimed from the sea and the wild lands tilled.

XXIX

A SON OF THE VIKINGS

E was a bright, blue-eyed, red-bearded young marshman, athletic and strong of limb, and long of wind.

A tallow-faced youth from the city stopped, and asked him in soft voice the way to the village.

He replied quickly, and, going on his way, remarked— 'I don't like them white-faced Londoners. I like to see a man with a brown skin, one who looks as though he could eat a jackass and a skepful of greens.'

'Would you have him eat the jackass raw?' I asked.

'Raw? yes; I've eaten raw beef and pork long ago a good many times, when I've been to sea. When we had our fresh stock come aboard, you see the chaps out knives, and cut off a slice of the boilings and put into their mouth, and off they go about their work. And that go high too . . . but that make men short in the temper.'

XXX

THE STRAY TURTLE-DOVE

THEY had bought him a new cage, and he seemed proud of it, for he cried, 'Cook is a rogue,' with a louder voice, and ate more maize.

He was a handsome bird, with his ashen upper parts and twy-patched neck and cinnamon mantel stretching down to his white under-parts, that led away down his tail-feather shafts, and on to their broad white tips.

Near by was the old box, latticed with rough pieces of lath, wherein he had spent the bitter winter. His cage faced the cold south-east face of the sky, where, in the winter nights, blazed the frosty constellations.

His only covering had been a coarse-webbed sack thrown over his rude cage, yet leaving two lath spaces open to the cold, keen breath of the winter; but the yellow maize, ripened beneath the tropical sun, seemed to give him all the fire he required to battle with the frigid season, and the laths kept the hungry rats and stoats from his warm body.

Already the bird had taken the daughter's place, for she

months, when the strange turtle-dove flew down to the clump of cottages by the mill, and sat upon a post turning his regards to the poultry feeding on corn before the door. The miller passed and the bird heeded not, so the old man turned and looked upon him, for it was November, and most turtle-doves had left the fen-land. Still the bird did not move, so he approached it and tried to take the warm feathers and elegant creature into his brawny fist; but the bird, like a coy maiden, eluded his grasp and dropped lazily to the ground.

Mindful of the ways of maidens he ran in for his lures, the maize and an eel-net, and scattering the grain before the bird, he saw it eat Then to capture it was an easy task, and to imprison it in the hastily made cage the natural consequence .. And now it is as one of the family, and no price is fixed upon its head, nor ever will be by the old miller.

XXXI

THE MAY MOON

THE burning sun had worked all through the mild and lovely day, swelling the buds of the elms, unfolding the curved hawthorn-leaves, brightening the pink clusters on the show currants, springing the daisies, paling the cuckoo-flowers, and adding a brighter lustre to the flaming yellows of the marsh-marigolds.

At sunset the orb went down a golden ball bulged at the sides, the yellow turning to a blood-red in the greying sky, and for a moment the tossing reed-tassels and the glowing red ball formed an enchanting natural decoration. But, lo! as one watched, the soft greys began to steal over the distant trees, the moon arose, facing the sinking sun, and the two bright spots in the heavens were throwing their magic lights upon the scene at the same moment. But as the sun sank below the sloping reeds the landscape all around was seen hung with cobweb grey, a curtain so light and airy that the smoke rising from the near vessels passing without the sand-hills seemed coarse and dark in comparison.

peace, and softly wreaths of grey vapour arose from the
heated waters and ronds, and formed floating vignettes of the
most delicate, flawless, gossamer-like materials, and the silence
was so profound that for a moment the world seemed to
doze; but this still scene, with its delicate mist, only seemed
the clearer to accentuate the sounds coming over the distant
plains, the hoarse barkings of a watch-dog at a marsh farm,
the voices of children playing in a distant village.

Then these sounds died away, and the birds' evensongs
filled the air ; cuckoos called from the mists, all making that
peculiar rolling heard in the courting season , reed-buntings
sang low, short, sweet notes, nor was their music drowned
by the plaintive calls of a male lapwing or the laughing of a
snipe, as it circled round and round over its nursery.   There,
in the solemn silence, one could hear the curious distant
'aho—ho—ho,' as the lowing herd walked slowly across the
marsh-wall homewards.   Again there was a solemn silence,
broken presently by a whistling redleg, the short notes of the
elegant yellow wagtail, and cheerful twitterings of the sedge-
warblers.

Softly the whitening mists entirely veiled the fading
distance—mills, villages, farms, trees were gone, and though
the ships on the sea were just ringing their evening bells, still
the birds sang on ; and as I listened I heard for the first time
that year the ticking song of the grasshopper-warbler sung
beneath the waxing moon that was silvering the gossamer
wrapped round the horizon

But gradually the birds settled to sleep in their misty

beds, though many were restless, and awoke at intervals to twitter or sing a sleepy note; but as their little throats were hushed in slumber the frogs took up the chorus, and they crooned sleepy lullabies to the birds far into the night, till the sleepless cocks called from farm to farm whilst the May moon reached her plenitude, and was in a second of time already on the wane—so peaceful are the workings of Nature.

XXXII

THE WAYS OF WOMAN

JIM, the big blue-eyed, sandy-haired marsh-man, had been paring the banks of the parallel dikes, and cleaning out the green, slimy, cloth-like masses of lamb's-tail all the March morning, working hard in mud and slimy gutters, so that the stupid Irish cattle should see the dike-edge, and not tumble in when they went to feed along the rushy shores.

As the yellow evening sun turned the landscape to gold, Jim shouldered his scythe and crome—for his work in the dike was done,—rubbed down his great wrinkled tall boots with a wisp of dry rushes, and went walking home in the golden light to his cottage among the bare apple-trees, stopping on the way by an old dike wall to unearth a buried hare caught in one of his looking-glasses the night before.

When he reached home, tired out and later than usual, his hard-working wife, neatly clad in black, with a clean,

As the big man entered, the woman looked up and said, 'Where have you been all this time, you great piece of a man?'

'Been? To work. Where do you think I should have been?' answered the marshman shortly.

'Have you cleaned your boots?'

'Yes; rubbed them on the mat,' Jim answered as he walked across the clean-scrubbed brick floor to the airy back-house, where he began to wash.

The quick-eyed wife watched the great fellow walk through the room, and seeing some bits of mud left by his boots, she shouted out—

'I thought you had cleaned your boots, bor!'

'So I did,' mumbled the man through his towel.

'Yes—that looks something like it on the floor; come you in and look at the bricks.'

'Ay; I shall have to pull my boots off in the shed, and shift them altogether before I come in, I expect,' grumbled Jim.

'Yes; and that's the proper place to do it.'

'Oh, all right,' said Jim, coming in and sitting down to the table on which the savoury bloaters gleamed.

As they were eating their simple meal, some one knocked at the door.

'Come in,' cried the wife, and a stout, black-faced man opened the door and stood hesitating in the doorway.

He was Jim's brother-in-law. As he would not enter, his sister cried—

'Well—come in, don't stand there; it is cold.'

'But my feet are dirty,' said he, looking down at his boots.

'Oh, *you'll* never hurt my house—come in,' and the fat man stepped in and dropped awkwardly into the nearest chair, while a grim smile passed over Jim's weather-beaten features.

'I come to ask you to lend me your brewing-tub,' said the man.

'You're welcome,' said his sister.

'Well, I'll take it now, if I may; I'm in a hurry.'

'Yes, it's in the back-house, go you and get it.'

The stout man tramped heavily across the room, leaving heavy mud-flakes all along his track, and they heard him take the tub and disappear through the back-door.

When the door was shut Jim looked over to his wife, his eyes twinkling, and said—

'Yes, that's how you do. You are always down on pillgarlic; but if there be a stranger come to the door, it is, "Oh! *you'll* never hurt my house."'

'Of course, a stranger isn't one's husband.'

And big Jim smiled—somewhat bitterly.

XXXIII

YOUNG LIFE

WHEN Man disturbs natural laws he gains in one way and loses in another.

I watched a goose, with her brood of fluffy yellow goslings three days from the shell, eating grass and following the gander across the rough dry ground. They were quite healthy, for the farmer had never fed them from the first; but there were only three goslings, because the careful housewife had taken each egg as it was laid, to keep it safely from the hands of the farm-boys, and the shells had become dry and hard by the time they were returned to the nest of down and straw when the full complement was laid, so that the native warmth and moisture from the sitting goose brought off only the last laid eggs. But even the three children were far too large a family for the hissing gander, for he would stop at times in the bright sunlight, and give the little yellow head nearest him a terrible peck with his hard and spatulous bill. I remember seeing a proud old gander kill his only son in this way some years ago upon a rushy common, and the mother in nowise resented the crime.

As I walked into the lamb-pens, where the woolly orphans of the flock were fed from a large baby's bottle, the little flock of lambs ran to me, but when the shepherd's boy appeared with the glistening bottle, they left me and ran to him, following him round the yard as they would have done their dam—such is the *love* they bear their feeders, a fact worthy the regard of streaming-eyed sentimentalists.

I saw the shepherd whetting his knife, and then suspected the glass bottle was used upon this occasion merely as a decoy, for soon the shepherd had seized a strong young tup, some three weeks old, and holding it in his arms with its back towards him, I saw the old shepherd with a deft cut amputate the sac, and pressing the glistening root-like testes from their beds, he seized each one between his teeth and drew it forth by the root, as one draws a young radish from the ground, and the lamb wriggled once or twice, and was placed upon the ground a eunuch. Then with a quick stroke of the knife the creature was deprived of its tail, when it walked out of the shed and stood in a dazed fashion in the sun, looking back, as if expecting some further surgery The little animal shivered once or twice, and its hind-quarters seemed to contract and draw up, its ears falling backwards on its stretched-out head. Then it moved a few steps forward; its hind-legs were partly paralysed, and seemed to drag after like the legs of the wounded lion in Assyrian bas-reliefs. A few drops of blood fell on to its fleece (sentimentalists should weep here); but alas! as the boy appeared with the feeding-bottle the lamb forgot its little woes,

and ran after him with ears shot forward and loosely closed
mouths, as happy as the proud Bantam cockerel that flew with
a rakish air upon the quickly greening hedge surrounding the
sheep-pen.

In a paddock, two of the ewes I had seen the previous
night lying, great with young, in the moonlit straw, were
now suckling their new-born lambs, one of them rearing
the little offspring of a fever-stricken ewe as 'lovingly' as
her own children; and such is the 'filial' love of animals
—a mere instinct that compels them to love, and cherish,
and follow a glass bottle as they would their own dam,
and such the parental love of the gander, that is ever ready
to peck his intrusive offspring to death; and such is the
maternal love of the brute, a mere instinct, that compels
the female to protect the young creatures in her sight,
and to offer them the breast for her own relief. But in the
fulfilment of such instincts the bird and brute may feel,
proportionately to their instincts, as deep-seated a satisfaction
as when the young mother suckles her babe; the young woman,
however, is richer than they in experience and emotion,
and she is sicklied o'er with foresight and retrospection,
attributes the sentimentalists would ascribe to the lower
brutes. But such are justified of their æsthetic emotions,
and Landseer is their god, while some—not sentimentalists
—prefer to worship the lions of an unknown Egyptian

XXXIV

BLACKTHORN WINTER

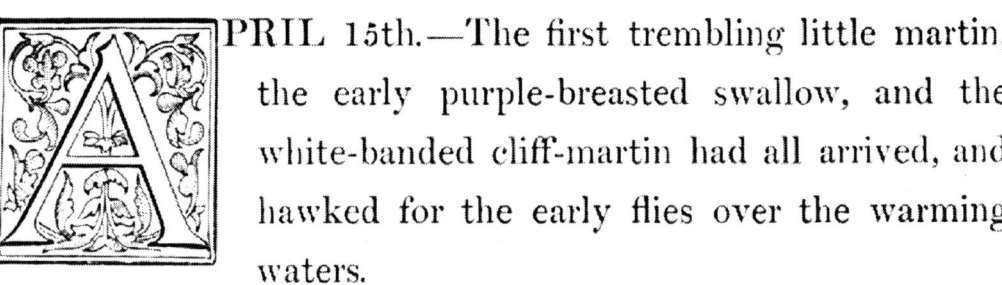PRIL 15th.—The first trembling little martin, the early purple-breasted swallow, and the white-banded cliff-martin had all arrived, and hawked for the early flies over the warming waters.

In the budding coppice the speckled mavis and hen blackbird sat on their precious eggs in their warm nests, and even the tomtit was weaving his green bower in a hollow tree, and in the high leafless elms overhead the rooks were sitting on their blue eggs. Down by the water-side the pike and perch had deposited their eggs, and left them to the sun to hatch, near the shallows where the water-rails and moor-hens were already hatching their rusty-spotted eggs in warm nests made of gladen and sedge, as they sat still contemplating the wavelets lapping up to the low shore.

The peewit could hear the snipe bleating over the hole in the ground where his mate's dark blotched eggs lay; yet winter was to come, though the blackthorn in warm, cosy corners amongst the grass was powdered with the first white petals.

the bright mercury thread in the glass thermometer to blood-heat Yet the nor'-easters came with force, snow-squalls racing in speckled clouds athwart the brindled marshland, contending with the storm and dancing before the reeds driven before the wind ; for as you looked at the storm, with your back to it, the colour of the marshland was deeper and richer, and your heart danced with delight as your ears were filled with the roar of the approaching squalls, and the quiet crackling, like the beaded skirt of a dancing-girl, as the snow-wreaths fell into the muffled river and melted

The racing squalls grew faster and more furious, dancing over the reddish rushes until they faded away into a bright luminous haze, where the marsh and sky met in a light halo shining before the reed-tassels potently swayed to and fro by the storm. And throughout the wild scene piped the restless redshank, for his is the voice of the snow-spirit on the marshland ; and as you turned your face sideways, with your right cheek to the storm, following him as he darted through the strong lines of white, you saw there was a deli cate grey and luminous distance in that direction, and clouds of snow swept like smoke across the distance, and the mills and cottages loomed and rose into the grey, formless void, looking like fairy palaces and spires floating on a luminous mist, for the snow-squalls transfigured the distance, and you saw a novel and lovely mirage across the brindled marshland.

And so passed the brief blackthorn winter, leaving behind frosted figures on the dead grasses, and white streaks upon the rushes

XXXV

A LITTLE LEARNING IS A DANGEROUS THING

THE town of Reedmere was blessed with a vestry, and according to Norfolk custom the date for an Easter vestry-meeting was duly fixed. When the day arrived the ground was white with snow, and a fierce nor'-easter was blowing, bringing snow-squalls in from the North Sea.

The newly elected vestryman walked through the storm to the church. When he stepped inside the cold, gloomy vestry he found the place deserted; indeed, the white, smooth snow in the churchyard bore no footprints.

As the new vestryman knocked the snow from his boots the surveyor arrived, then the timid squire, who was so reserved that busybodies did not know he kept a heronry; indeed, his breeding-place for these splendid silver-grey birds was not given in the usual catalogues. After him the overseer arrived and began to talk of the coal strike. Four out of five vestrymen were now present, all sitting with long pinched faces in the cold cellar-like room, waiting for the

the primitive saints blazoned in crude colours in the windows. The timid squire could stand the discomfort no longer, so he deputed the overseer to go and call the parson.

After some delay the overseer returned with the parson, who wore his buskins and hat, attired as if bound for a journey. As he walked in and shook hands with the squire, nodding to the other potentates, he said breezily—

'Oh, I really forgot there was a meeting; I was just going to start for the station, but the snow is rather deep.'

The squire coughed in a nervous manner, and rubbed his tingling hands as the parson sat down before the simple table, apologising, before beginning business, that the stove had not been lit—that should be done without fail the following year. Then looking over to the new vestryman, he said unctuously, 'Mr. James, we have held these meetings amicably for twenty years, and I trust nothing will mar our pleasant relations. We generally decide quickly on our new men, and we will proceed to elect our overseer, surveyor, and parish constable.' The new member said nothing, as the old gang were returned, and the dear old times were kept up

.   .   .   .   .   .

But the new vestryman had been elected on to the school board as well, and when he found the parson, as he expressed it, 'bossing' the school board as well, his conscience pricked him, as we shall see.

For a time came when the town of Reedmere had to decide upon technical education, since they were offered it, and the parson, as chairman of the school board, called a meeting. His daughters—highly 'cultured' young ladies, as they thought, fresh from South Kensington—were present.

And when the question arose as to what should be taught the peasantry, the eldest girl said precisely—

'We should elevate the populace by teaching them wood-carving.'

'Yes,' seconded Lucinda, an amateur water-colourist, 'and painting.'

The new vestryman fidgeted in his chair, for he was one of the people, and knew their mind.

'I think, sir, the populace would prefer rough carpentering'

'Yes, yes,' stammered the squire, 'I was thinking so myself. It is, I th—in—k—k, a work of time to teach poor people an art—even in amateur fashion. I beg to propose a meeting be called and the people be allowed to choose their subject.'

The simple and inexperienced, artless young ladies protested. However, the squire's motion was carried, and the wise people chose for themselves, and the subject was gardening, or 'horticulture,' as the new vestryman called it with a touch of pompousness.

XXXVI

THE COCK AND HEN

T was cool there beneath the rustling willow-leaves, from whose green faces the sunshine poured and fell on the dry, sandy soil, where the hens were basking. There were spotless white Dorkings and silver-laced Wyandottes, black Minorcas and the blue ladies of Andalusia, prolific in eggs.

But most of all my attention was attracted to a proud young Dorking cock, who had just espied a magnificent Langshan hen, that morning arrived at the farm. She was feeding beneath a willow when he saw her for the first time, and he was transfixed. Then he looked about him doubtfully, then sidled up to her and began to pick on the ground, casting cock's-eyes at her, but she would none of him, and kept her back to him. Seeing she was cold, he at length dashed forward and began to pick by her side; but she raised her crest, loosened her wings, and lowered her head in a threatening manner, quite throwing him off his guard, for he began to pick nervously at the ground, still keeping one

stood for a moment, looking after her, with one leg raised in air and his claw half-closed, finishing up with a loud crow of disappointment or—derision.

I have seen the same spectacle enacted between man and woman.

XXXVII

VOICES OF THE NIGHT

N you wander on the lush marshland on a still summer night beneath the starlit sky you will hear all round you the voices of the night—singing-birds. The canary-like sedge-warbler babbles in joyous song from yon sallow islet in antiphone to the sweeter-voiced and more precise reed-warbler, who makes the reed-bed ring with his song; suddenly, close by you, sounds the mysterious clicking of the grasshopper-warbler, and whilst you are listening, wondering at the strange song, a nighthawk flutters by over the reed-bed shrieking, and startling a water-rail, that begins to whistle softly, 'whiö, whiö.' Then follows a lull, and you hear mice working in the stuff by your side; and as you listen a corncrake begins his cheap-jack-like vesper on yonder green marsh; but his distant voice is chorused by the harsh 'frank-frank' of a heron, and the plaintive plovers calling 'three hillocks a week, week arter week,' as they gleam to and fro in the rising moonlight, awaking the red-legs that fly round and round their nests whistling 'a-love, a-love,' and as you stop bewitched with the wild marsh notes a

droning snipe wheels round in the starsome sky, laughing wildly as he drops down the air over his sitting mate. Then there comes a lull, mayhap, and suddenly a cuckoo begins to call from yonder planting reflected in the still mere, reminding you that you have only ten years to live an you believe the old woman's rockstaff; and the cuckoo seems to waken the ringdove that begins to croon to the moon gliding through the trees of the water-side carr, where you may hear the watery tribe of teal and duck whistling and cackling to the moon And a marsh-owl screams, and the frogs begin their intermittent chorus, hushing, mayhap, just as a water-hen calls a loud cr—r—ook, or a coot flies with cries from his nest, driven forth by a hungry stoat. A horse snuffles near you, and again peace descends on the marshland, and only the cry of the sea is heard away over the sand-dunes. But a scarce-moving cygnet passing slowly up the river like a ghost recalls you to the fulness of the tide of life by night, and a bird's cry in a stoat's grip recalls the tragedies of the night. Even when the marshes are frozen the voices of the night are not hushed. 'Frank' still calls, peewits wail, and flighting fowl fill the cold night with their voices. And you go home assured that nothing is constant but change, nothing certain but death.

XXXVIII

A GOOD DINNER

 DINED *en friand* to-day on one course, and that a great, green, black-backed bream, weighing *in puris naturalibus* nearly two pounds; he was as full as a Lynn mussel in season. But I will tell you all about it.

The day was miserably cold and cloudy, freshly arrived flycatchers and reed-buntings were trying to sing, but their song was ineffectual, and they soon joined the other birds, and hid in the warm, dry marsh stuff and water-plants. I was staring at a primitive and very rickety pumping-engine, the torn sails of which were pumping off a feeble stream of water into a slimy trough, and fast getting in the doleful dumps, when an old man appeared—my old friend of the moleskin cap, old velveteen jacket—an heirloom of his keeper days,—and an old pair of trousers with a leathern knee-cap on his left knee, for he often knelt on that knee to dig out the young moles.

Coming up, he took his coarse-webbed sack from his back, and, opening it with grunts, he shot forth on the sod several great green black-backed bream and two small

tench, for the large tench were not yet out of the mud,—
the weather was too cold and the skies too clear. He was
proud of his catch, for they were all full fish, weighing
from one to two and a half pounds each.

It had been his birthday the day before. I had made
him happy. He had been sorrowful for a moment when I
smiled as he told me it was his birthday, though at the
time he said nothing. but in the evening he handed me,
with a reproachful air, an old parchment with lavender
letters, his mariner's certificate, made out on April 8th, 1828.
As I read the crumpled 'Mariner's Register Ticket,' No.
212,676, and looked into the weather-beaten, honest old face,
that day sixty-four years old, I felt reproved and sorry for
my light banter.

However, the bag of fish, netted in a private water for
me that day, showed there was no smouldering ill-will, and
after a glass of ale at the wayside inn, where we talked fish,
I returned with my booty to the boat, and Jim took the
bream aside, and beneath a budding willow, where sat a white
wagtail among the ivy leaves As he was scraping off the
scales and skinning the big bream—for you must flay your
bream,—a merry-faced girl came up, turning her bright door-
key upon her shapely forefinger

'What have you got there?' she asked, unabashed, and
as I looked into her face I found one eye was a beautiful
brown and the other as black as a sloe; and as she returned
my look she seemed to laugh a double laugh with her different-
coloured eyes She was lively, and would help to clean

the fish, so we all skinned them and scraped the backbones white as a hound's tooth, and then, placing them in salt and water for some minutes, we paused and chatted with the variegated-eyed maid. But she was equal to us; and when the fish was rinsed, and drying in the cool breeze, she ran off, avoiding the awkwardness of a farewell.

The fire was roaring, and a hard juicy fish, with the roes of five others, were soon sputtering and sprinkling the boiling oil on to our hands, stinging them like pricks of needles

. . And then to the feast; the rich brown outside, the tender steaks, and the delicate brown flakes with their crackling were before us, that is the titbit of the bream. 'Twas a delicious meal; and after every vestige of the flesh was gone I fell upon the red-brown roes, and when I had finished this delicious dish I reflected on the insolence of the salmon-killer, who smiles when you talk of eating bream, and on the all-knowing cockney who prefers to eat bream in summer.

Your bream is at its best when the kingcups blaze on the river-side and the first sand-martins are fluttering over the bistre water for the early sluggish flies—that is the bream season. And if you cook him as I have told you, this is a dish for honest men, such as shall turn you fishermen the very next year as soon as the speckled thrush begins to sing among the ivy leaves, for at that season the black-backed bream are savoury with the perfume of river water.

XXXIX

THE FIRST MARTIN

A CALM rested upon reed-bed and stream; the glowing heat-waves seemed to linger over the moist soil, whence they floated reluctantly into the unknown.

Suddenly a small bird flew with wary flight athwart the burning azure; it was the first sand-martin that had burst into the sleeping scene from the sounding sea.

The little traveller skimmed down to the peaceful river, and began to hawk eagerly for the indolent flies, as it had done a week before on some African stream, beneath a blazing sun. And yet but four days of moist-eyed April had gone.

The news soon spread from mouth to mouth through the village that the first 'swoller' had come. His arrival would be registered in the weekly paper on the coming Saturday, and many a heart beat more quickly as the news went round, for every one was as eager as this most eager of martins to pluck of the fruits that the season would bring, for in the spring-time life lusteth after all the goodly lusts of the flesh; all the world migrates, in heart if not in deed,

XL

A WHERRYMAN—HIS WATCH

WAS leaning over the starn after some water and my watch-glass broke, but that went all right for some time. A little time after, when I was winding on it up, the cog flew out of the wheel, so I took her to pieces and onscrewed the big winch, like the winch what you wind the sail up with, and took my shutting-knife and cut some more cogs in—that was soft—that hadn't nothing to do with the wheels what keep the time.

'Arter I'd so done, I took and broke a pin and put it through the cog-wheel, for I'd lost the totty little screw what held it in, and that used to go too; that went several days, and one day the pin flew out so the cog-wheel get out of the gim-cracks; so I took her home and gave her up for a bad job—she want frying. She'd no face on her, and her inside was out of order; she want to have a box o' liver pills.'

XLI

A QUIET AFTERNOON

PRIL 22nd. The wind had died away so that each reed slept and all the lagoon was silent as death; the very houses seemed to sleep, and only the voice of the frogs croaking in the warm, still air could be heard, when a young woman in a scarlet jacket came and sat by the water-side with her two daughters, and the flute-like tones of their laughter floated over the mere.

When sitting on the bank the young mother began to play her sweet, drowsy music, filling the afternoon with her silver voice, as she played her concertina under the thin, grey sky.

Her husband, who was hoeing the foul grasses between the ridges of young blades of wheat, stopped in his work, and, resting on his polished hoe-handle, looked across the water towards his young wife, and as he watched his eyes softened, and a look of love, sweet as the music, spread over his sunburnt features. And as the young woman played and sang, her children gambolling round her, a sigh escaped

scene and the rude music, he walked across to the other side of the field and determinedly resumed hoeing up the foul grasses.

As I listened, the water-birds seemed to feel the influence of the music, for the water-hens began to call idly from the reed, and the snipe laughed and circled lazily above us; all the watery tribe seemed filled with the influence of that soft-aired afternoon, for it was an afternoon meet for love and poetry—languid and intoxicating. The little white wag-tail hopping by to the water's edge looked on curiously and sleepily, waiting probably for an opportunity to return to her grey-spotted eggs, nestling up there on the top of an old willow crowned with ivy. When the music stopped the lazy smoke-clouds curled away above my boat-head, seeming to move more quickly, for they had hitherto seemed to circle in mazy figures to the tune of the simple music.

XLII

AT A MARSH INN

IS dusty coat was resting on the cart-shafts slanting to a bit of warm, sunshiny green land, where a pair of geese fed their yellow goslings; his pony was in the cool, dark stable munching a ninepenny feed, and he was in the ale-house reading the daily paper and sipping his jug of six-ale : for since he was a rider [1] his time was his own.

After a time he finished his paper, and, pushing it aside, looked curiously at the first drowsy flies sunning themselves in the dusty window, and the voice of the great black-backed bees buzzing from the petals of the saffron-hearted crocuses blazing in the garden beneath gave a pleasant music to the scene.

The shrewd and jocose rider felt the quiet calm of the country spreading over his inmost being, so that his face wore a more kindly, humorous expression when three great marshmen entered for their mid-day pints—it was hot work cutting litter on the dry marshlands that day.

After passing the sele of the day and calling for beer,

the sunburnt men, with their long boots and stone rubs thrust into their bright shining leather belts, seated themselves at a polished deal table and began tapping with their big round finger-nails on the board—too shy to open the conversation.

Suddenly the bluff-faced rider roused himself, shaking off his drowsy reverie, and turning to the nearest man he asked cordially what was the latest news of the village.

'I dunno,' said the man. 'Passon Johns hev to pay two hundred poun' to Maria Asseton for breach o' promise o' marriage.'

'He's a nice bewty,' added the dark marshman; 'they'd far better have let the old curate keep the living when old Passon Gilbert died'

'But won't they take his gown away from him for this?' asked the rider.

'O noa, they won't never interfere with a passon without he commit murder, and they see him do it,' said the dark marshman bitterly.

'They're a pretty bad lot, then, about this part of the world,' suggested the rider.

'Bad, yes—as the old 'un. There's that Seaward passon, he wor in the bankruptcy court. He used to preach temperance at the Seaward and come here and booze up reg'lar. When he was bankrupt his bill for spirit was over £30; and then thar's old Passon Mason of Seaton—he died o' drink; so did Passon Gilbert; lor', they're pretty near all alike.'

'Why, bor,' said the dark man, 'when I used to live at

Acla our passon used to go every Sunday to preach in another village near by, and he allus allowed himself a quart o' beer before preaching.

'One Sunday he was drinking his quart at the "Horse and Groom," and he got tossing for another, so he had to pay for two quarts instead of one. He come late to church and drove right slap into the porch.

'So the clerk he told him the people had near all gone.

'"Call 'em back, call 'em back," he say, "I'll soon put it into 'em."

'Time he was getting ready and getting his gown on, a few drawed in. He began drawling, and muddled through the prayers and began to preach; and he fell off to sleep. Time he was preaching the people all went out of the church, except the clerk, and he shook him and say—

'"They're all out, sir."

'"Fill 'em up again," says he, kind o' drunk, thinking they was talking of pint-pots.'

And the men's laughter drowned the humming of the bees in the crocuses.

XLIII

ON THE STUBBLE

E walked over the stubble, passing some men in tanned slops loading freshly felled tree-trunks upon a waggon, to a sunny corner of the field near a coppice, where a man was gathering the sweet white chips into a roughly corded sack, whilst a bright sulphur butterfly fluttered through the naked stoles, and a mavis sang its love-song in the budding branches above.

Around the bright part of the field lay some ewes with their woolly lambs, whilst others fed upon the scarlet beet. As the farmer looked round upon his flock, he remarked that some of his lambs were too fat; the ground yellow maize had fattened them too quickly for the butcher's fancy. An old ewe with dishevelled wool hobbled by, scarce touching the ground with one foot.

'Ah!' muttered the farmer, raising his slender, crooked ash stick, and running forward he hooked the halting ewe by its hind-leg, she running on terrified for a few steps; but he was upon her, and had her on her back against his stout legs, and was examining the proud-flesh budding under her hoof, whilst a curious speckled houdan cock and his harem strutted by, glancing curiously at the surgeon and his patient as they passed. The ewe's head seemed squarer and more full of character as I viewed it in its new position, its moist nostrils dilated, its great bluish eyes rolling anxiously, as the surgeon pared away the hoof and exposed the raw disease. Once or twice the animal winced and struggled, but the insensible creature seemed to suffer little pain, and to be resigned; indeed, there was an expression of resigned patience upon its characterless features.

And when the sore was dressed the brute struggled hastily to its feet and hobbled off to a tooth-sculptured beet and began to eat—its only joy.

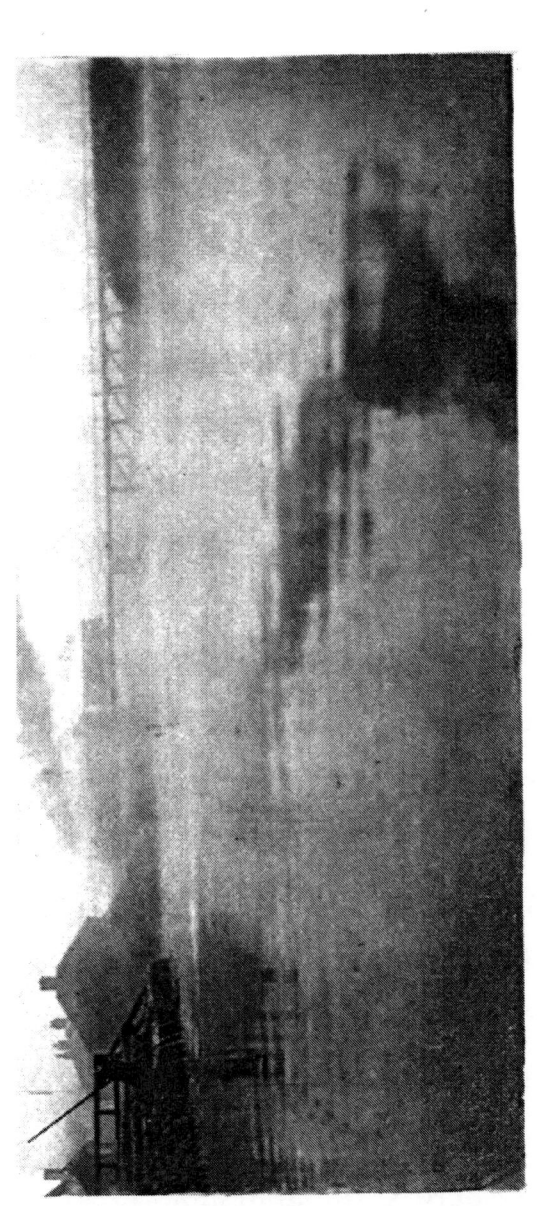

XLIV

A NOCTURNE

FTER a burning day and lemon sunset, grey wreaths of mist began to rise and float over the dusky river, where the still reflections of the fairy-like trees slept under the bright moonlight.

As the afterglow paled in the western sky, the pale round silver disk of the moon, quaintly marked, shone brighter in the pale blue sky, and burnished the clouds of white mists now floating over the brimming water-ways and gliding softly over the marshes, muffling the rough gorse-plants and spiked rush sentinels in a diaphanous cloak fine as cobweb. And now the quaint, reed-thatched cottages peeped above the silvery sheet of mist, and all the landscape was a fairy scene, the feathery tracery of trees peeping forth and silently contemplating the caps of the walls and the picturesque little garret windows of the cottages, all watching silently across the marshland, their bodies veiled in vapour.

And as I gazed upon the mysterious night, I heard the villagers leave the gossiping corner on the green, and the

urchins their play, and then followed sounds of muffled
mirth as lovers parted at their lonely doors, and all was
still in the village; only the cry of a restless child reached
my ear from the sleeping hamlet.

Still the mist wreathed and swept above the river, blown
by the softest of night-breezes, and a dog bayed at the moon,
in a lonely farmhouse across the whitening marshland, for
a rime frost with delicate fingers was painting the mysterious,
reposeful landscape All the tribe of birds seemed to feel
the chilling influence of the frost-crystals which now sparkled
in the bright night light, and the nocturnal and mysterious
silence was broken by the low, far-off whistles of the redshank, the wild spirit of the marshland, the contented and
comfortable call of the night-feeding water-hen, as she ate
amongst the gloomy and broken old gladen stalks, and the
plaintive cries of the green plover, to which the sportive
cock replied by whistling and circling through the misty
moonlight, calling to his hen, 'Three lovelocks I seek—week
after week,' and bustling about her as a young and ardent lover
about his fair mistress. When he settled upon the marsh
and folded his bronze-green wings, there was a lull in the
voices of the April night, and all nature seemed to sleep pro-
foundly, except the mist, which glided mysteriously down the
bosom of the river. But this slumbrous peace was disturbed
by the childlike cry of a young lamb that the frost-
whitened ground sent shivering to his dam, and the invisible
snipe began to drone through the pale grey-blue dome—
the drumming sounding in the still night more like the quick

beating of hard-pinioned wings than it ever does in the day-light; flying up in silent curves and dropping sideways, laughing like summer lambs, the anxious cock-bird circled round and round the patient hen-bird, who was perhaps nestling closely over her four large speckled eggs in a grassy tuft below him, her warm body keeping out the dark mists and frost-scales. Mayhap she slept on the white marsh, and he, like some lover, gazed upon his lovely bride, who dreamt all unconsciously of his worship at the shrine of love, and youth, and beauty. . . . In the next lull of the night-watch I too fell asleep, and all was still.

XLV

A NORTHERLY BREEZE

THE lagoon was girt on the leeward side with a wreath of foam whiter than the swans who were lost in the driving, scudding mist-clouds flying over the ruffled water before the cold northerly wind.

As my boat beat up to windward, close hauled, her white sail pushed aside by the cold breath of the May breeze, a large craft loomed through the mists, and a stack of hay flashed past quanted by a man with a long fir pole. The strange craft disappeared as it had come, through the grey mist. Never a boat did I see; it was as in flood-time, when houses and haystacks seem to float on the face of the waters.

The white mists thickened quickly, and silently began to hide the miserable stone cottages, as my boat beat up past the mist-shrouded beacons in the channel.

As I put my boat about, the mist that had swept in from the sea hid the shores, and I was in a formless waste where 'twas idle to make for port; so, shooting up head

strip of an island set in a necklet of foam far whiter than a swan that fed beside it, and there I rested; for this reed-crested haven was to me like unto a palm-fringed islet to the castaway mariner.

Nothing could exceed the delicate grace and beauty of this strip of landscape, set like a gem in a misty pool.

In less time than it takes a swan to swim ten boat's-lengths the mists cleared, my sail filled, and I once again realised that the expression of a landscape is as mutable and fleeting as the flash in a woman's eye.

XLVI

THE NEW WHERRYMAN

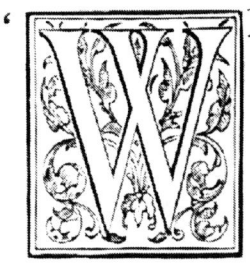'HAT d' you say, bor?' asked bluff Bob, a forty-year-old wherryman, of his new hand, a dreamy lad brought up on a lone marsh-farm, as they lay at Catfield Staith waiting for the corn.

'I was saying, old Bob, as how I thought I'd be lucka, for the fairies hev been to ours onest; they come and cut some wood, and 'nother time they come and mended the old man's boots; he see'd 'em: for he had the power. One of 'em had a bit of leather, and t' other a lapstone and all.'

'That's a rare cuffa,[1] bor; I suppose their feetings lay fleet, eh?' said old Bob, with a sneer.

'Well, bor, I dunno; all I know is, the ole chap he's got a fairy stone what he picked up on the ma'sh—a round white stone that is.'

'Ay, I expect your folk are dranting[2] folk, aren't they? quiet as the ground?' said Bob sarcastically.

'Well, they keep a slow fire and burn a rushlight, as folks should do,' answered the lad with spirit.

'Yes, lively as a lingthorn,[1] no doubt,' jeered Bob. 'But drop them old rockstaffs and give us a song.'

'Not I, I 'ont drop 'em, I believe in 'em. Why, only last year-day old Sal Harmer and mother was sitting talking over their teas at ours, and the teapot was 'twixt them both, and both on 'em made ter take it at the same time, and blow me if mother ain't in the family way again !—so that rockstaff be trew.'

'All right, bor, do you believe in 'em ; be all of a dudder [2] when you hear the ghostesses. *I* ain't. I never see nothing worse than myself; but give us a song.'

'Wal, bor, what shall us sing? Shall it be " Gathering the blossom on the old thorn-tree," or " Ella Barnes "?'

'I don't know ; how do they go ? '

'Wal, the fust go—

> 'Gathering the blossoms from the old thorn-tree,
> Sweet-scented blossoms from the old thorn-tree,
> The hours I have passed away,
> In the merry month of May,
> A-gatherin' the blossoms from the old thorn-tree '

'Wal, bor, I don't think a sight o' that; how do " Ella Barnes " go ?'

'That go—

> 'I knew a dead dairymaid
> Named Ella Barnes
> She fell in a fit as she stood by the churn,
> There came in a shower of spiders and fleas,
> And she swore the old churn had the cattle disease.'

---

[1] Star-fish   [2] Tremble

Old Bob roared with laughter, and said—

'Give us that, bor; that be proper, that be.'

'I like t'other best; that's only nonsense,' pleaded the lad

'Damn you, sing that "Ella Barnes." I don't want no poetary ; I want summat comical.'

So the lad sang 'Ella Barnes,' old Bob roaring and joining in here and there.

At last the tumbrils came up with the corn, and the wherry was filled, the hatches put on, the sail hoisted, and all ready to start down the river.

A few moments afterwards Bob came aboard, rubbing the beer-froth from his lips, and, letting off the sheet, the great sail filled, and the wherry glided down the river. As they sailed down the stream the lad got the mop and began to mop across the hatchings.

'What are you arter there?'

'What's up there, old Bob?'

'Why, sweeping them hatches crossways; don't you know that's onlucky?'

'Is it, then? So you believe in rockstaffs arter all.'

'On a wherry—that's different,' said Bob dreamily, and the lad smiled.

At length the wind dropped, and the lad was told to quant. He managed it fairly for him, and when they got into a fair reach the lad laid the quant down and proceeded to wipe all the mud off with a piece of sacking.

'Blow me! what are you arter now?' called Bob.

'Cleanin' the quant, o' course,' said the young chap.

Bob looked dumfounded.   At length, when he recovered his speech, he said solemnly—

'Boy, you are too much of a gentleman—I *mane* it—for this here trade.   I shall ax the master to put you inter the office when I get back.'

And he did; for Bob was a good sort at the bottom, though extremely 'shucka.'[1]   He didn't like being imposed on, and had an idea most people were impostors; but when Bob found they were genuine he worshipped them.

[1] Shaggy

XLVII

THE TIDE-PULSE

T was my fortune once to have to watch the ebb and flow of a tide on a wide lagoon, and delicate work it was, for a sixteenth of an inch rise or fall was invaluable; indeed, it was tide-recording on the most delicate principles.

All who have never observed Nature's mysterious workings take it for granted that a tide ebbs and flows at regular intervals with invariable and mechanical regularity, and after reading such superficial statements as are to be gleaned from Physical Geographies, the *naïf* student might learn much from feeling the pulse of Nature's arteries as they softly ebb and flow up and down the face of a deal stick.

The lagoon was a wide, shallow expanse of water some eight hundred acres in extent, connected with the sea by a river some twenty miles long.

When I first undertook the task of carefully noting the rise of the brine-water, I discovered that it took considerable time for the great heart-beat of the ocean to drive its life-

anchored. As I notched my stake and got it level with the slack, some time behind the almanac time at the harbour bar at the other end of the river, I lit my pipe in the warm April south-easterly breeze, which rose, hastily blowing the idle lagoon into ripples, and raising the water in my little drain a quarter of an inch. One squall heavier than the other actually blew the water from the other end of the lagoon, quickly raising the water over half an inch; but as the wind dropped the water fell back, but not so far as it had risen, for the great body of the lagoon was rising—the legitimate rising of the tide.

With the top of the tide the wind shifted from the westerly to the north, and away the tide began to run in the cool glittering evening, and an inch was gone in a moment, and I feared me my little drain would empty But with the setting sun the wind dropped, and by the bright starlight I saw the local disturbance had re-balanced itself, for the water was rising as it returned from the far end of the broad; but still it never returned to high-water mark, and kept on slowly but surely falling, imperceptibly if looked at steadily for a few moments at a time, for the subtle forces of Nature often work so slowly that the eye cannot follow the changes, except at intervals: it is like watching the small hand of a watch.

It was nearly midnight when I returned to the tell-tale stake with a lantern, the water-hens calling and moving warily on the rond, looking for the eggs I saw them robbed of that afternoon. And there was the water; it had fallen

over an inch; for upon a wasting moon more water runs
away than rises, and *vice versa.*

The next morning, in the crisp frosty air, we had a good
tide up, a surprisingly good tide up, for we were beginning
to feel the full effect of the nor'-westerly winds that had
blown three or four days previously on the North Sea; that
wind always raises the water of our lagoon, much to the
delight of the spawning pike that I saw sluggishly basking
on the hair-weed. Up it came, a full, bounding, healthy
tide, creeping up the white face of the stake, and rising an
inch and a half, for there was a good head of water on the
lagoon at the time; for, mark you, if the sou'-easterly winds
had blown for long down on the North Sea our lagoon would
have gone very low; indeed, once it went so low in these
winds that a hunted deer and some adventurous horses
walked across the wide but shallow sheet of water, and
obviously, when such was the case, it required a greater head
of water to raise the spent waters of the broad.

So day after day I took the tides, the flycatchers singing
at my tide halts, eulogising Venus, and the wild note of
coot and water-hen accompanying my registrations. Sometimes my lantern revealed mists like wreaths floating over
the water, at others sparkling frost-crystals; and on these
night-watches I heard the rats feeding on the banks, small
fish jumping in the warm waters of the dike, wild-fowl
feeding in the reed-beds, and restless dogs and fowls barking
and crowing in the farms around.

And throughout that tide-taking I noticed some cottages

by the water that burned a light in the windows all night long, and I marvelled, for the poor seldom waste. In one cottage, I heard, was a sick baby, in another lived a curious old man, whose ways were wanton, and in the third lived a newly-married couple, and from my inquiries I discovered that many a cottager is timid at night, and burns a candle to keep off ghosts.

With the tide, the mysterious actions of that young couple worked all night long in the watch-lamp   .

By day many quaint old water-side folk drew down, and told me what they had seen in their days.

One wherryman told me he had drunk fresh water out of the river at the distant sea-port, and salt water as high up as Heigham Bridge Another told me he had seen the tide run down for three days and three nights through Yarmouth Harbour, though the water had risen a little at flow—indeed I had seen as much myself

An old fisherman told me how they often caught sea-shrimps in the lagoon, and one old man said he had caught a sea lampern, 'all gay as a Poll parrot,' about four pounds in weight, and another had seen a sprat, a veritable sprat, caught on the 'fresh-water' lagoon, and many old bearded men with gaunt eyes spoke of the number of dead fish they had seen when, after long spells of dry easterly and south-easterly winds, the wind had suddenly shifted to the nor'-west on the German Ocean, and sent the hot spring-tides right up on to the lagoon in such an unadulterated form that the fish were killed; for your bream and perch thrive better, if anything, in a brackish water, and pike can live in such water comfortably, but the 'salts,' none too sewage pure, kill them.

And when my task was finished I learnt, after all, that the Geographies were correct: the tide ebbed and flowed in even my far-away capillary, but by my watches by day and night I learnt the life of waters, their passions and caprices, their variability and uncertainty, and the dull truth that the water's ebb and flow became a living reality. What the school-books tell us is no more than if a physiologist were to tell us that the heart beats and drives blood through our circulation, and that so we live. These twain facts are fundamental and never-changing truths, but upon the everlasting tide-pulse in man and ocean depends the constant change and uncertainty that give life its zest. The twinkle in the lovely maiden's eye is but like the local blowing back of the waters, but of what profound interest it is to men with sane hearts and sound heads!

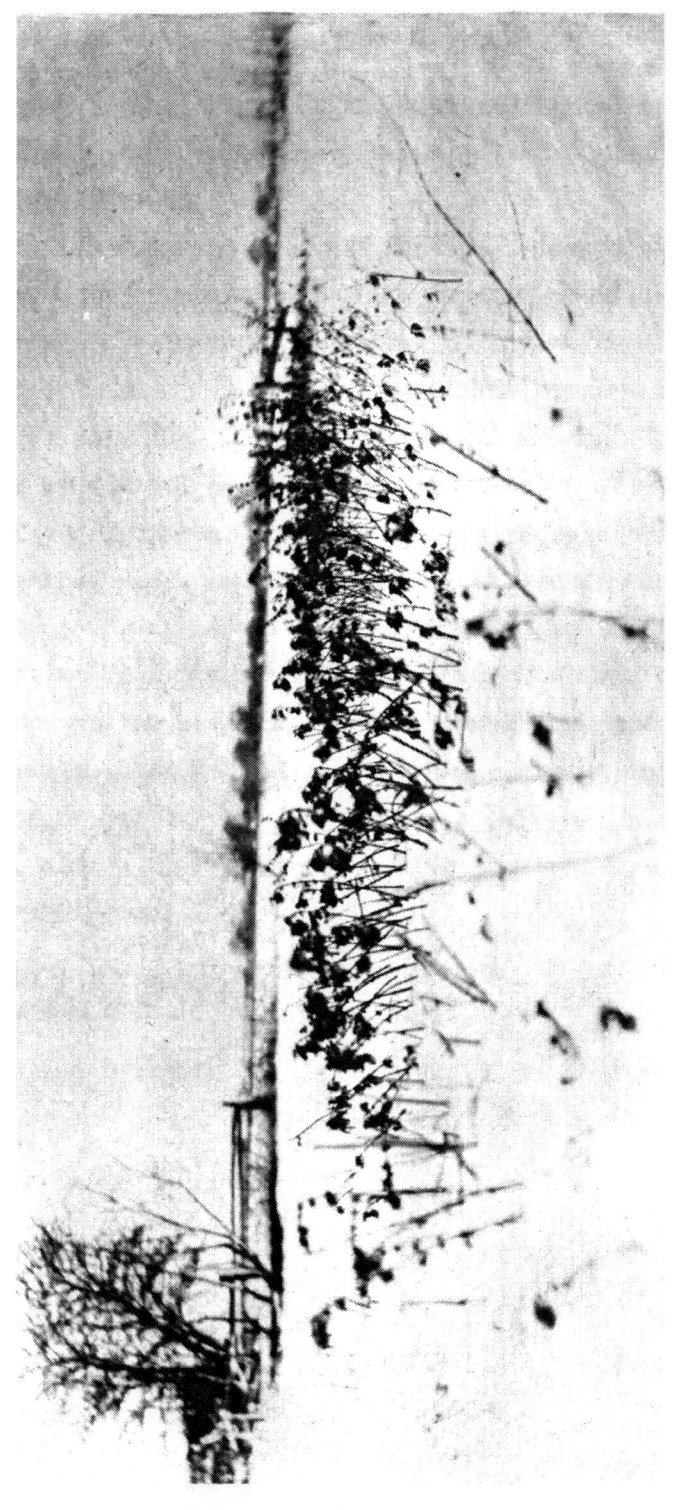

XLVIII

RURAL FELICITY

HEY were cousins; one a carpet officer who kept all his old dinner-invitation cards stuck with studied carelessness round a huge mirror —need I say more?—the other a red-faced farmer who had come down in the world and intended going up again.

Formerly they had been thick, but now things had altered, and as they talked of the worst side, each standing on his own land, the one the squire, the other a small farmer, his tenant—

'I wish you'd leave that long stuff on the marsh adjoining the coverts; it hasn't been cut for twenty years, and my game like it.'

'I'll leave it for ten pounds a year,' says the other.

'You speak very cavalierly; you must forget who I am.'

'No, not in the least; you are my cousin, and you forgot to send your carriage down for my wife when she arrived, and I had to borrow a farmer's cart to bring her up to the

'Yes, yes; circumstances are altered, you see. . . . Well, will you let that stuff remain ?'

'No, not under ten pounds; are you going to pay it ?'

'No, certainly not.'

'Here goes then,' said the tenant, taking a box of matches from his pocket, and, stooping, he lit the long dry stuff to windward, and in a few moments the marsh was a field of flame, and the squire had fled in the smoke and flying cinders.

　　.　　　　.　　　　　　　.　　　.

Nine months afterwards the squire's tenants had all given notice to quit; he would not lower his rents, as he was living far beyond his means   When this happened he had to come down in the world and let his hall with its shooting.   Then he went round to his cousin, shook hands heartily, said they had always been friends, and that he looked forward to coming down and visiting them each year, for he was going to live in the City.

The good-hearted cousin said nothing, but thought the more.

XLIX

THE VILLAGE BIRD-STUFFER

HIS ideal was naturalism, since he was a good observer and sportsman; his works at times came up to his ideal, as his magnificent old black epauletted cock heron with sable plumes and white cuirass proved, as he stood with his spear-like bill drawn back and one foot raised—ready to strike an eel. His water-hen, too, *ran*, and his snipe lay sunning themselves, one stretching his wing like a turtle-dove. On a dark velvet ground his corncrake crept.

As he stood and prepared a frame in his little room, decorated with roach and bream skins, birds bound up with white threads, and the tools of his craft, his wife brought a small parcel covered with postmarks and placed it upon the table, withdrawing silently.

Stopping and putting his work aside he took up the box, and, opening it, he drew forth a ruffled and bloody little fire-crested Regulus. A sigh escaped the man as he smoothed the tiny body, for he knew the rarity of the bird; but sigh

so, placing the little body—weighing some seventy grains—beside him, he wrote to his fowler:—

DEAR JIM,—The bird—a fire-crested wren—all blood and postmarks, arrived safely   Do you mind not using a ten-bore gun and duck-shot when you shoot these small birds?—Yours,   ROBERT OWEN.

And he smiled placidly as he sealed the envelope.

L

SUNDAY AFTERNOON

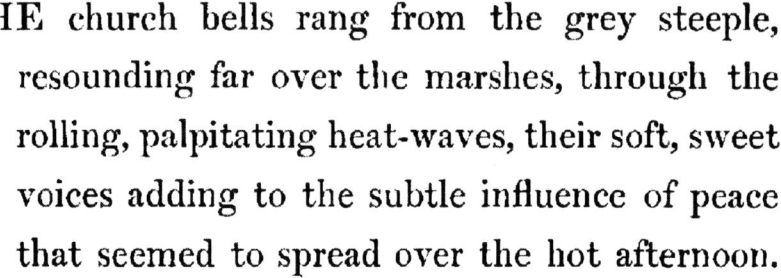HE church bells rang from the grey steeple, resounding far over the marshes, through the rolling, palpitating heat-waves, their soft, sweet voices adding to the subtle influence of peace that seemed to spread over the hot afternoon. Not a figure was to be seen, though the flash of a red skirt passed like a meteor through the dry branches of the leafless hedgerow.

When the church bells ceased a starling sitting on the highest point of a mill-sail took up the music and sang softly, more quietly than a mavis, though some of its sweet notes at times recalled his neighbour; but often the note was that of a sparrow, or at times the teams' trappings set to music. Presently the starling too ceased his love-song and flew off into the blue; and in the sleeping white afternoon quietness two lads came from a cottage with long ash-poles, fitted with snares, for they were in search of small pike basking in the dikes, or, mayhap, a larger speckled fish in the delirium of spawning. They went along the dike-side,

saw a fish, when, stopping, he noiselessly dropped the slim wire into the water, and standing back passed the noose gently over the drowsy, unsuspecting fish, jerking it suddenly on to the hot marsh grasses, where it beat out its life, silenced for ever.

LI

THE BEWITCHED PIG

'MOR! that pig is witched,' said Jimmy to his mother at the mill one morning in July.

'Witched, eh? wring her wallers—the old warmin.'

'Yes, she's witched,' reiterated Jim.

'Well, now, boy, do you cut off her tail and cold the blood in a gotch and bring that ter me.'

Boy Jim did as he was bidden; and that night Mrs. Evans stopped the keyhole with bread-crumbs, pulled down the blind, put the pig's blood to stew on the fire in a pannikin, and sat with her son silently looking at the fire, she with her finger on her lips.

Presently there was a noise at the door, and the old woman looked eagerly round, and then, signalling to her boy, she pressed her lips with her fingers almost till they bled.

But the scared boy said—

'What's up, Mor?'

'Dang you, it's all done!' said the old woman in a rage. 'If you hadn't spoken they'd a bursted, or else they'd been standing by the door in the morning dead, but now it's no good; do you go to bed, you fule, and get up early and kill

LII

THE WIND AGAINST THE LAW

HE fishing-boat *Viking* was drifting over the sullen North Sea with a westerly wind at three o'clock one autumn afternoon. Three hands stood on deck—two Barton men and one 'Paddy from Cork.'

'The wind is eastering,' said the sandy-headed Norfolker.

'Ay, bor, it coming against the law.'

'What ever will that be?' asked Paddy.

'You'll see, sure enough,' replied the first speaker.

'Busky, oh!' called the watch, and at once all hands came tumbling up on deck.

'What's up?' asked the skipper.

'Wind against the law; it's blowing from the east now.'

'Ay, so it is; we'll blow back over the nets if we don't do something. That ain't blowing tew hard; no, I'll try it,' said the skipper to himself; and aloud, 'We'll out the little boat, Joe Lame, and, Teddy, you go along in her.'

It was now dark, and the tide had begun to turn, and

along the long line of nets, stopping at the last and shining their flare. At the signal, the captain cut the warp that tied the fleet of nets, and the vessel began to blow back across the nets towards the little boat, the boat's crew throwing their trat or tow-line to the skipper in the fishing-boat. The fishing-boat was then brought up head to wind, and the warp re-bent to the pole-end, and the vessel allowed to 'tid' on till morning

And Paddy now knows the meaning of 'the wind against the law.'

LIII

A COUNTRY CHILD

QUAINT, dreamy child was blue-eyed Gladys. She was never like other children, for she was always reading some fairy-tale and talking to herself in the old garden, where the peaches ripened and the corn-flowers bloomed. One day she would be a fairy prince, peering through the gnarled and bunioned branches of the old espalier-trained codlin apple-tree; another day she would be a dainty princess, as she walked beneath the beautiful Kentish morella trees, pranked with blossom; or perhaps she would be a bear roaming through the evergreens, seeking for a child to devour.

Every one loved Gladys, she was so kind and nestling; and you may imagine the commotion in the little household that lived in the rose-embowered dwelling beneath the elm- and lime-trees, when Gladys was found weeping bitterly on the schoolroom floor one fine August day, just as *her* peach-tree had ripened its first luscious fruit. None could pacify her, not even her father, who generally soothed all her cares.

golden head in her two little hands, her whole being shaken
with passionate grief. Beside her lay a book. At length
the tears were dried; and that night, as the tender child lay
in bed, her mother pressed her gently to tell her trouble.

The little girl looked serious again, and said softly—

'Mamsie, I read in a book to-day that as I had given my
love to another I am ruined. O Mamsie dear! I must be
so wicked, for I have given my love to ever so many people;
you, and papa, and Jane . . .'

'O my poor child! don't think any more of those silly
books; they are only fairy stories.'

But it was long before Gladys could be soothed, and
longer still before she was fully persuaded that she was not
a wicked, ruined girl.

As Gladys grew older she got more curious, wishing to
know the reason of everything; indeed, her early romantic
state of mind had developed into a more scientific state;
mayhap the deceit of the book that told her she was ruined
for giving her love to another had disgusted her buoyant
and emotional nature.

At any rate, when Gladys's youngest sister was born
Gladys was anxious to know whence the baby came, and
none would she listen to save the professional nurse; she felt
instinctively that nurse was the authority.

Day after day she set about cultivating the nurse's friend-
ship, bringing her chrysanthemums from the garden and
maiden-hair fern from the greenhouse, for little Gladys was
great friends with the young gardener.

At length one day, when she went for a walk with nurse, she asked her—

'Nurse, where do babies come from? where did Zoë come from?'

'Why, from under the cabbages, of course,' said nurse sharply, immediately changing the conversation.

.   .   .   .   .   .

That night after dinner Gladys's father called her into his study and scolded her more than he had ever scolded her before.   He was really enraged with her, for she had (so her friend the gardener, who was equally enraged, told him) pulled up *every* cabbage in the garden, young and old, Savoy or Red Dutch; *every* cabbage had been ruthlessly pulled up and cast upon the ground.

The more the father scolded the more silent was she, and her father, in a rage, at last sent her off to bed, himself breathing forth threats of all kinds, for he was genuinely angry.

.   .   .   .   .   .

But nurse went and soothed her, and asked her why she had been so naughty.

With brimming eyes she kissed the kind woman and said—

'Why, nurse, I was looking to find a baby under one of the cabbages: you said that was where they came from.'

And the nurse hid her smiles by hugging the child to her ample bosom.

LIV

A DAY WITH THE RATS

E met at the marsh mill,—old Bob the rat-catcher and alert Potter the marshman, Peter, a water-spaniel, and his brother Toby, together with a long-legged puppy *in statu pupillaris*, who smelt wildly at every hole and blustered with bark. Old Bob had his ferrets in a sack over his shoulder and a mole-spade in his right hand, Potter had a long-barrelled gun, his 'old Bessy,' and I took my eyes along with me.

It was a lovely spring day; the snipe were clamouring and the sandpipers calling in the shallows, whilst over the dead and gleaming dunes the wash of the sea could be heard. As we walked across the rush-marshes the pup would sniff at every inconsequent mole-hole, at every little pile of fur where kestrel or stoat had feasted. On our way we startled several hares, Peter or his brother darting after them, barking loudly; but the hares soon left Peter and his brother behind them, and Potter itching to loose his gun, but 'twas forbidden. On a marsh by the sea we saw the brindled herd moving slowly round and round, pushing each other clumsily, and I looked at Potter. A wicked gleam was in his eye, for he knew well what it portended,—a hare in a snare, probably set by Potter himself;—but I was not too curious.

When we left the marsh (Potter had slipped behind) we came upon a thorn-hedge leading to the sea—a dry 'deek,' where all the undergrowth had been cleared so that no rats might cover there, for the farmers know well clean hedgerows mean 'no rats.' As we skirted the marshes lying inside the wind-sculptured sand-dunes we came upon a bright stonechat on a rail watching a flock of voracious starlings feeding on the newly turned land. Old Bob, who had taken Potter's gun, fired into the black flock, which arose with a whirr, cripples dropping till all were lost in the blue. Old Bob wanted food for his ferrets, so he bagged some half a dozen of the slain, putting the last in his bag as Potter came up, and said, 'One old Sally.' I turned and noticed the cattle had dispersed, and Potter smiled blandly.

At length we came to a pig-sty standing by a pile of faggots, where we were to rat. Behind the pig-sty was a patch of garden—newly dug, terminating at the hedgerow that separated the marsh garden from the marshland. There were four pigs in the sty, and they grunted and stared at us curiously.

Old Bob took off his bags and began pulling out some of the faggots, pointing to the places where the bark had been eaten off. Then he went into a shed behind the sty and found a pile of roots, many of them eaten hollow by the vermin, but never a rat was to be seen

Old Bob then went to his ferret-bag and brought out a fine buck polecat ferret, and a white ferret, and put them into holes beneath the sty, whilst Potter stood on the marsh with his gun fixed on a spot between the large holes and the hedgerow, and the dogs stood at attention between the sty and the hedgerow; they knew where the rats would bolt. Soon there was the squealing of a rat in the ferret's grip, and several rats' heads appeared at the different holes, and many bolted for the hedge, and then Peter and Ned were busy barking and seizing them by the middle of the body, shaking the life out of them, and there was an uproar in that quiet garden,—the rats squealing, the dogs barking, and Potter's gun going off every now and then as a rat crossed his mark.

The polecat ferret had meanwhile got his rat by the throat, and old Bob drew the pair forth, taking the still living rat from the ferret and throwing it on to the open ground. The ferret darted after it and seized it; the rat began to squeal, but the ferret kept turning him over and over, regardless of the squeals, until at last the rat gave up the ghost, its sharp chin and cruel eyes turned up to the blue sky.

In a short time not a rat was left by the pig-sty or faggot-heap, for the ferrets went into the holes and came forth empty-mouthed. But nine large rats lay dead, and the escaped were in the hedgerow. The ferrets were then put on

to the hedgerow, and as I watched the big buck polecat it
began to snuff the ground like a hound and run along the
hedge, soon entering a large hole. Presently I could hear a
rat squealing in the hole near by, and, sure enough, his tail
was just visible hanging out of the dark gallery He had
evidently tried to back out and was caught.

'Pull him out if you can,' said Bob, 'and see the sport'

So I seized the great tail and pulled with all my strength,
but never an inch would the ferret yield ; so I renewed my
efforts, and suddenly away came the skin of the rat's tail in
my hand.   I had cleanly peeled its tail, yet the ferret had
not given an inch   It was useless to pull then, so we waited,
and presently the great ferret came forth with his prey.   In
a short time there was not a rat to be seen or turned forth,
and fifteen lay dead.

We returned along the bare hedgerow into the marshland, and jumped the dikes on our way home, scattering the
flocks of chaffinches, bramblings, and greenfinches and land
buntings feeding on the cultivated marshes, and finding the
wings and feathers of two 'mocking rooks'; relics left by the
rats that had 'cleaned them up.'

On our return to Bob's cottage he opened a rat, discovering
the steaming entrails, which brought forth a family of ferrets
to feed.   They closed round the corpse with blazing eyes,
arched backs, and ears laid back, and began to feed, and the
old doe crunched the head and shoulders with fierce appetite,
whilst old Bob smiled satisfied, and Peter and Ned lay on
the wall looking at him.

LV

COTTAGE PROPERTY

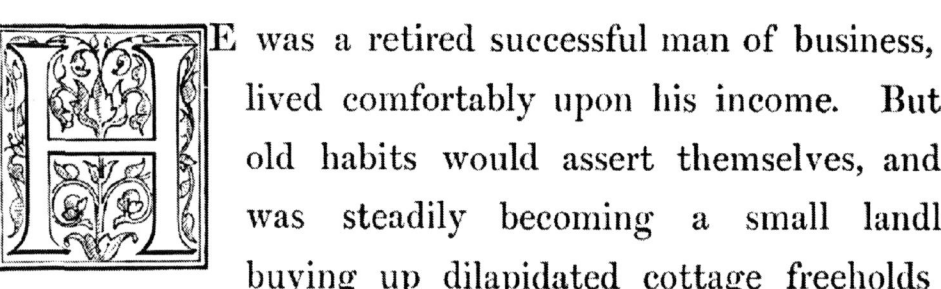E was a retired successful man of business, and lived comfortably upon his income. But his old habits would assert themselves, and he was steadily becoming a small landlord, buying up dilapidated cottage freeholds extensively for the purpose of increasing his own garden, for he gardened so carefully that lemons ripened within twenty yards of the river.

He always opened a credit and debit account when he made a new speculation, and balanced his books as methodically as a cashier. He had theories on pumps, and his books taught one lesson,—'Never buy a cottage unless the pump be in working order.'

Voilà !—

To rent of cottage, one year . . .	£3	8	0

To repairing well, scraping down same; bottomfying do . .	£0	14	0
One new wooden vat and ironing up . .	1	5	0
New suction-pipe to pump, and fitting .	0	13	0
One new leather flange; new cleek, one new bucket, one new box; stuffing, packing, fixing box, 3 lbs weight iron, screws, and 3 bolts, .	0	8	3
Repairing all iron-work	0	5	9
Repairing wood-work and painting same . .	0	2	0
	£3	8	0

LVI

LOVE-TIME

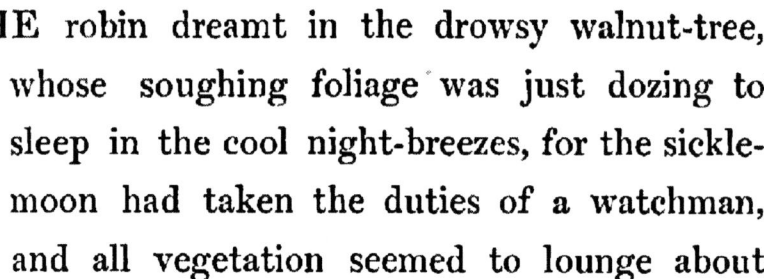HE robin dreamt in the drowsy walnut-tree, whose soughing foliage was just dozing to sleep in the cool night-breezes, for the sickle-moon had taken the duties of a watchman, and all vegetation seemed to lounge about the garden in unbuttoned garments; the leaves rustled like a loose tag against a pretty instep, the white flowering anemones wore their nightcaps, the vinery had been shut for the night, and already the moisture of the budding grapes was gathering in dew upon the large window-panes.

Puffs of fragrance from the sleeping flowers were carried through the dark and silent alleys amongst the evergreens, straggly elms, and shady sycamores.

The hens were roosting in their painted coops; even the bats had gone to their beds, filled with flies gathered beneath the dozing trees; but a white muslin dress floated like a moth adown the trees, and all the music of the night breathed from her stately form, as, gliding along the mossy tree-trunks, she sped through the garden, filled with vague longings and romantic thoughts—for the warmth of the evening had breathed into her heart the desire for love.

LVII

THREE WRECKERS

T was a sun-white July day on Winterton beach. The sandhills shone like burning volcanoes, and the heat-rays floated like smoke as they rose behind the marram-fringed dunes. A soft breeze was blowing, and scarce rippling the clear blue sea, which looked like a mill-pond.

The white slops of a group of sailors sitting by the edge of the sea gleamed like snow, and their purple shadows were sharply outlined on the sand. There were three of them —old men,—one, wearing an old sou'-wester, had a white beard and white curly locks that made him look like a sea-rover. The biggest man of the three was a burly old fellow with a red face and a yellow sou'-wester. On his left sat a dark man with black eyes and a felt hat. They looked at the sea and at the clear, still sky, and the burly one raised his telescope and fixed it on a passing brig.

'A Norraway wessel,' he said sadly.

The dark sailor-man sighed.

'I wish a b——y big steamboat would come ashore now,' said the burly one, fixing his eye greedily upon a passing collier.

The old white-haired one laughed, and looked at the

LVIII

BLUE, AMBER, AND GREEN

THE May-day showed a fresh and radiant land-scape fanned by a cool yet mild south-westerly breeze, tempered by the warm sun that poured down on the labourers dike-drawing, bronzing them, whilst it deepened the green on the set blades of young corn that greened the furrows, growth scarce hiding a hare on her form.

All around the birds sang; the sweet-voiced yellow buntings in the blackthorns with their prickly sprays and wreaths of flowers; the pied reed-buntings on the greening sedge answered the sweet-voiced reed-warblers and shriller, flickering, butterfly-like sedge-birds; and the sentinel corn-buntings sang regularly their short, sweet songs on the top-most budding sprays of the hawthorn-trees;—every bird was vivacious in the ambient air.

But the verdure down by the lagoon wore a primeval freshness; and as I sat rocked on the blue water, with a row of dried amber reeds between me and an osier carr now in its young prime—for the catkins were burst, ripe for insemina-

lovely and delicate stretches of blue, and amber, and fresh green, my whole being was filled with satisfaction : the scheme of colour was so perfect, so delicate, so beautiful—for in such arrangements Nature surpasses the most cunning painter.   She is inimitable and unpaintable in her choicest, most delicate moods, and this the best artists have recognised, for, as Mr. Whistler has said, 'The artist is her master in that he knows her.'

But turn where I would, there was the colour-scheme of early May—blue, amber, and pale green.   I could see it in the sedge-leaves growing from the pulk, in the gladen shooting from the dead stuff on the mere, and in the young spear-like shoots springing from the rond, bristling with cut amber stalks.   There was this colour-scheme all around me, even in the blue sky, sandhills sleeping by the crooning of the sea, and far-stretching cornfields, now green with young blades.

But sweetest of all was the blue-eyed girl's face, with amber hair, that peeped archly from a green wreath of reed.

LIX

THE IRISH STEER

IT was a poor thing—the Irish steer with long hairy brown coat spotted with white, and scarred with scaly patches of ringworm; and the poor spiritless animal was feeding upon a lean rush marsh covered with a scant crop of darnel and water-grasses.

In one corner of the marsh an Irish youth was harrowing up some old stubble, for a reckless farmer had tried to get a crop of oats from the poor soil, and the new tenant intended sowing cole-seed and rye-grass for his sheep.

The boy harrowed and sang—

> 'The priest of the parish and his gallant men
> Came over the mountain to marry Rose Ann;
> There was Larrie, and Sheila, and twelve more besides,
> With their long pitchforks to welcome the bride.
> And we had annocks, and bannocks, and butter-milk galore,
> And fine oaten bannocks we had forty-four;
> And as for onions and leeks, we've enough of our own,
> And a lot of salt herring came down from Tyrone!'

Turning his harrow about and about, glancing now and

eventide, for already the burning sun had gone down behind broad spaces of rosy, grey, and yellow clouds, all reflected in the burning river-spaces separated only by a grey-blue forest of feathery, fairy-like trees, that stretched away round the course of the skyline from a rosy windmill whose sails sleepily turned in the drowsy evening, he finished his task.

As the harrower reached the end of his course he stopped, and looked along the rosy dike, uttered a hasty exclamation, and ran down the wall, his brightly polished boot-plates shining like silver against the grey. Running on, he stopped before the sad Irish steer, that lay helplessly in the black slime of the dike, on its left side, its head turned sentimentally upwards, with spiritless, pleading eyes and dilating nostrils, for the poor heedless animal had fallen into the water whilst drinking.

'Agra,' muttered the boy, as he ran away up to the farm and called the farmer, a big red-faced man, crying excitedly —

'Shure! a steer is in the dike, and it's dying!'

Farmer Elliot seized a single halter from the stable and ran down the reed-marked road to the marsh with two men.

'Ay, it's the Irish steer; the warmin's got no pluck—he just like the men, they give up at once!' he cried, as he placed the halter round the spiritless animal's head; and the three stout Englishmen hauled the creature by main force from its slimy bed on to the grassy shore.

When the feeble animal had recovered its breath one man took it by the two ears, another by the tail, and the third by its hind-quarters, and all pulled and shouted in unison Thus urged, the Irish steer rose trembling and shivering to its legs, having a shrunk and humped-up appearance as the slimy and muddy water dripped from its mottled coat, and affecting to be lame in one leg.

Shortly afterwards it began to chew the cud as if nothing had happened, for he saw he could no longer humbug any one.

'Trust an Irish steer to eat; that's all he can think about,' roared the farmer, as he rubbed the trembling beast down with hay.

'Now he shall drink,' he continued, as he forced a quart of warm beer with some nitre in it down the throat of the beast that shook itself feebly after the draught.

'Irish courage,' muttered the farmer contemptuously, as the animal's nose grew moister, its coat dry, and its legs firmer; and then giving the animal a final cut with the halter, he said—

'It's just like their breed; an English steer would have got out of that ditch by itself; but those Irish cattle give in at once when they get into trouble, and lie as if they had neither life nor might.'

'But, yes, you must keep masters of the Paddies or they'll bully you awful,' echoed the teamster.

The boy at the harrow was singing again—

'Now the bride she was dressed in a short body-gown;
It was made of the fashion—the tail hanging down.
Her stockings were wool, their colour was blue,
Her petticoat frills and her brogues they were new.
Now the bride she was tall, and comely, and fair,
As small in the waist as a two-year-old mare.'

LX

THE SPIDER AND THE FLIES

NE hot autumn morning I heard the flies droning and buzzing sluggishly against a dusty window-pane, which the autumn sun made look still more dusty as I watched. I remembered those sluggish flies were holding their love-carnival, their last orgies before the winter cold should kill them or render them too sluggish for love.

Like drunken rioters they chased each other across the dusty glass, embracing sleepily, and as sleepily falling from the backs of their drowsy lemans. As I watched I saw a little spider begin to spin his web in a corner of the window-frame. He was quick and active, and the trap was soon ready, but as he span his silken meshes he seemed to detect the drowsy and stupid state of mind the flies were in, the observant little rascal. Leaving the web, he ran lightly to that part of the pane where the flies were thickest, drew in his legs, and lay silent as death. He mimicked the flies so closely that from my chair I could not tell which was spider and which was fly. His deceit was soon rewarded. An

mounted on his back, and began to embrace him. In a moment the poor fool's lover turned and nipped the drowsy fly and carried him off to the web—dead. The little spider returned and renewed his arts, capturing many stupid flies in this way; others, however, were too much awake, and avoided this false leman.

And there are philosophers who say that to know the world one must have lived in cities; but seers may learn the ways of the city-bred in the wilds.

LXI

RAIN AND MELANCHOLY

WAS awakened in the night by the sad sound of the rain that dripped from my cabin-roof, and as I listened to the sighing of the cold easterly winds through the reed-beds, I seemed to feel why these night rain-storms and night-sighing winds make one melancholy—it is the extreme loneliness of the weeping storm.

Away, far away, on the wide, dark tracts of fen-land, the rain-spirit was suffering, weeping, and sobbing, and filling sleepless souls with strange musings, 'that melancholy is a deadly poison, more subtle than *aconitia*, more sapping than intoxicants.'

This disease of the mind, born in the morbid, soon becomes an epidemic, spreading over the emotional degenerates of a race, and sapping the nation's manhood, and woe to the land where 'sweet melancholy' has found worshippers.

Brave men may have such fits, the gusts and tears of a rain-storm may relieve their manhood bursting with woe, and their tears may, like lonely night-rain, become twice blessed, but such fits are in the sane but morbid moments to be wrestled with in *silence*, and—conquered.

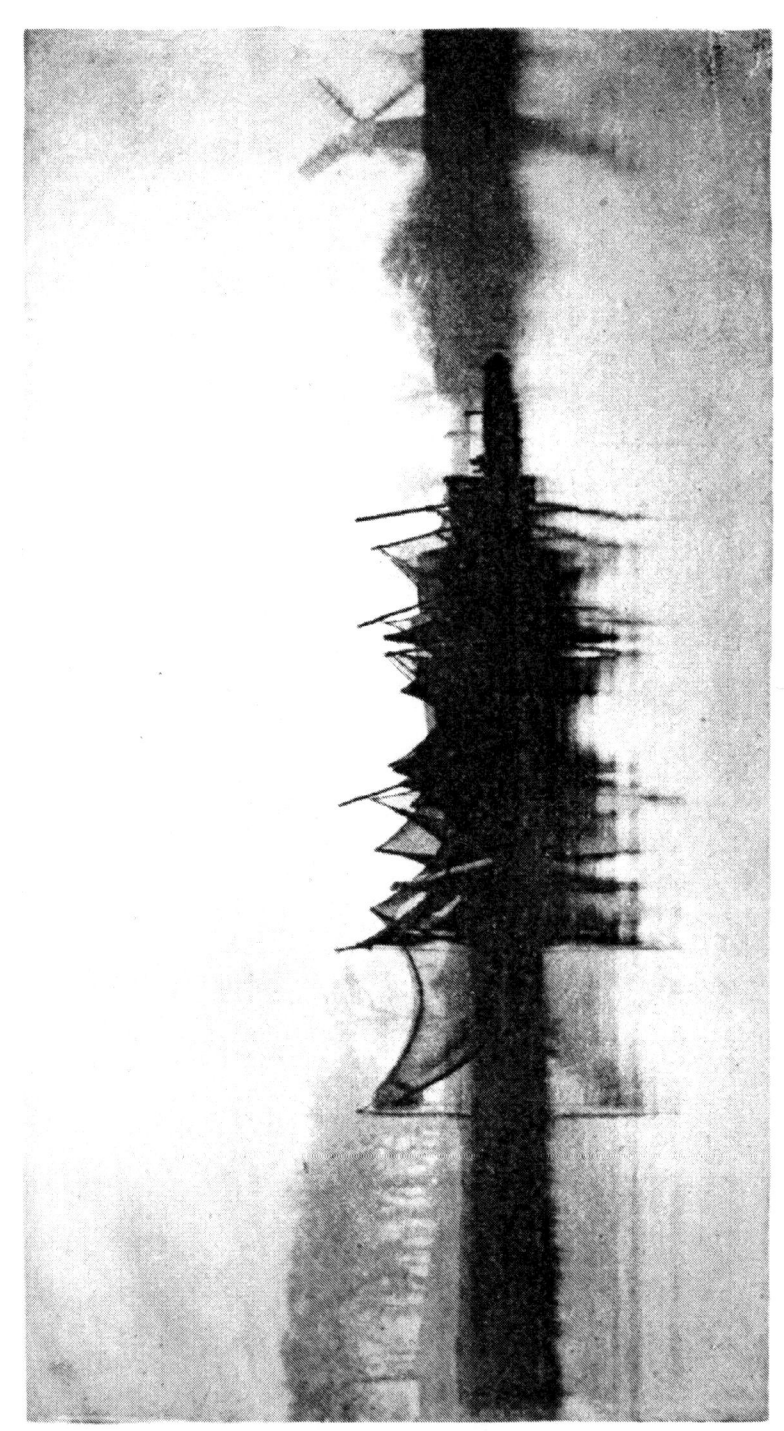

I drew my wraps around me and slept, and when next I awoke, poor, effeminate, weak melancholy had fled. I heard a crisp brushing and soft crackling at my window-pane; the savage, black, easterly wind had frozen the tears of weeping melancholy and sent them flying in white feathers to brighten the tearful face of the land, and as I looked forth on the whitened marshland, with its clumps of flickering reed-tassels, my heart was glad within me, for the white snow that had killed weak melancholy had smothered restless thought, for with her icy fingers she had simplified the vista before me, and so taken a great burden from the mind: such to me is the effect of snow.

The broad white snow-patches, with their beautiful clumps of reed in one corner, seemed to satisfy the æsthetic sense in its highest form, and lift from the mind the troublesome possibilities and thoughts aroused by the myriad details and life of the everyday scene.

Sweet, too, was the cold sheltered breath of the white storm, a peaceful antidote to the soft poison of the rain-melancholy.

LXII

OLD BEWTIES

THE wind blew a gale from the south, rippling the waters of the blue lagoon, raising long scarves of foam that blew into a dirty scum as they drove on to the oozy shores.

Across the stormy water an old man came, rowing with a feeble stroke in a stiff-boat steered by a black-eyed buxom lass—his young wife.

After they moored, they drained the stone flagon and went inland to visit their friends, she treading the green-covered staith like a queen, proud and conscious of her commanding presence.

The storm increased as a rough old amphibian, who, yellower than the lilies, had 'spat up the greater part of his liver' the previous summer, came down and reefed and hoisted their sail; he had been engaged to sail them back across the rough water on the lagoon.

They returned, the queen flushed with drink, and with them an old labourer and his wife, their friends. After getting

Whereupon the lively young wife said to the old labourer—

'You haven't kissed me, Sam'; to which he replied—

'No, but I ain't lost the job'

'Well, come on, bor,' she said, in her imperious way, and she raised her glowing face towards the toothless old man, who kissed her full lips right smartly.

The sail filled, the boat heaved on her side and bubbled through the rough water, the buxom girl waving her handkerchief, the old labourer with the protruding chin returning her signals.

Old Noll made three good boards, and their sail disappeared behind the budding willows and wavy reed-beds, but her splendid figure still remained graven in my memory

.   .   .   .   .

Next morning at breakfast old Noll was rolling to the staith drunk, his face covered with scratches, for he had rolled into several bushes on his way home from the village, whither he had piloted the queen.

All day he drank, when he was not abusing some stupid young men who were trying to row their boat with their sail up—crashing into the alder branches and exhibiting their folly.

By evening he was quite drunk and his pilotage-money gone, and as I looked out I saw him leaving in the cold night-rain in his marsh-boat, the innkeeper and a crowd of waterside wastrels hailing him as he knelt insecurely in his rocking boat and poled her down the dike grunting and swearing and shouting—

'April showers spring the May flowers.'

Still, habit was so powerful that we watched him essay the passage across the storm-tossed lagoon without forebodings, for he was too wise to stand up in his boat.

Away he went into the broken water, followed by a male swan whose roosting-ground he had passed. The bird was propelling himself along with nobly curved bill and flashing, angry eye; the drunken amphibian paying no heed to the bird till it began flying on the water, essaying to close with him. Then old Noll stopped in the beating rain, raised his hand to strike, and struck the bird with his paddle.

Noll reached the little post before his cottage door in safety, the swan returned to his beat, and the innkeeper to his customers.

. . . 'Noll will get the water springe,' muttered a fenman.

'He'll spin up a rare cuffa along with old Jenks,' suggested a reed-cutter.

'He'll be dead afore long,' muttered a sober-looking person in rusty black.

But that was prophesied of him some years ago, and he still lives.

LXIII

THE VOICES OF THE REED

APRIL 21st, 3 A.M.—Above, a grey formless waste of vapour; below, the silent lagoon stretching far away into grey pillars of mist; and through the moist morning air a clammy smell like fish. The night landscape had the appearance of the primeval world—for through the broad lagoon the dull masses of the reed-beds rose from the misty grey face of the waters, and the stillness of the sleeping waters was accentuated by the splashing of a fish in a reed-bush close at hand. As I stood with a son of the fens beneath an old dripping willow, there came a period of restlessness such as birds show through the night-watches; a water-hen—that embodiment of the voices of the waters—called 'cro—ook' through the heavy damp air, and then another called far away, and in a moment, from all sides, the water-hens took up the voice, and the quick shrill call of a coot finished the chimes, and all was silent for a moment save for the soft metallic croaking of a toad near by, and a deep mysterious noise like the breathing of some monster of the deep at one moment,

of a dancing-girl's at another. Then suddenly above this
deep regular undertone the cockerels began to crow all round
the lagoon, a dog barked, and the soft note of a swan feeding
close by could be heard; then there was another bark, and
the regular beat of the mysterious voice could be heard on
our right, the puzzled fenman listening, for the sound was
new to him; and as we looked on in the silence, through
the grey mists came a beautiful whistling chorus of red-legs,
their music softened by the mists; another lull, and the soft
and distant rustling of the dancers in the reed-beds took up the
soft lullaby, and no other sound could be heard save the call
of an owl, or splashing of some fish, or the twittering note
of an early sedge-warbler that sang its matins from a reed-
bed across the lagoon.

Again there was a lull in the voices of the night, but the
eternal and regular beat of the mysterious voice was there,
and all of a sudden the fenman's face brightened in the grey
soft dawn, and he said—

'It's the wash of the ripple in the mud,' for a soft
genial air was blowing from the west, the life-giving breath
of spring.

As we stood gazing at the formless grey landscape, and
listening to the mysterious voice of the reed-birds, a lark
fluttered from her grassy bed on the marsh, and lo! the mist
began to lift, a pale blue colour crept into the sky, the reed-
tassels were defined and the distant trees and shores of the
lagoons showed grey, sharp, and clear, and in a few minutes
the soft, mysterious music in the reed-beds was drowned by

the larks and mavises who awoke a few minutes later, and martins began filling the dawn with their chattering voices, answering some snipe and lapwings, who laughed and called each other.

And in less than a quarter of an hour the poetry of the night was gone, the daylight had arrived, and a cool breeze blew over the face of the waters,—a sweet humming sound being the last word spoken by the voices of that mysterious night.

LXIV

A MAY MORNING

THE morning broke fine, with the softest, sweetest breath blowing on my right cheek, the sailor's wind-gauge, and the wind was westerly.

About nine o'clock the delicate lilac and green marshland, set in a frame of lush enamelled kingcups, blazing above their green heart-shaped leaves; in brief, the poetical landscape recalling a Matthys Maris gave place to a Corot, with its bright distance,—for the low formless sky had softly parted, and the May sun streamed on to the distant cattle and mills.

As I sailed slowly down the river a man was sowing broadcast, walking steadily up and down the ridges, casting the grain with his right hand, and carrying in his left a peck measure, from which he replenished his stock. He walked along to the music of the land-buntings, perched on the budding willows, throwing the seed with a sweep that brought his tanned hand before his peck, where it hung for a moment ere it swung back like a pendulum till it reached

able to see that Millet had exaggerated the action in his famous picture; sowing is a quieter operation altogether, more deliberate, and in no way fussy. A roller was following the sower, pressing the seed into the soil—not a plough, as Millet has drawn it.

For the wheat-sowing they carry a measure hooked on to a girdle before them, and sow with each hand alternately.

As we sailed along, startling the ewes from the green marshes, and passing dead lambs drowned in the dikes, we came to a dike on the banks of which grew the pale cuckoo-flowers, and then we saw several ewes on one side of the dike and their anxious offsprings on the other, bent on attempting the watery passage; and thus it is the young and over-anxious lambs are drowned, for by a bad arrangement on some of the marshes the flocks can get on to the walls to feed, as well as upon the levels.

As our white sail glided past the frightened flocks they ran away startled, but every time a ewe stopped—many of them having a proud mien—the young lambs ran to their teats and tugged vigorously for a time; then the milk flowed and their little tails wriggled with comfort as they drank their warm sweet breakfast. And I saw one lamb run to the wrong teat, and, hastily giving it up, run round and seize the other, for young lambs and pigs know their own sides, and even their own teats.

Sailing past the smouldering piles of burning twitch-grass, we anchored by a four-year crop of sedge and reed, and went ashore to watch the birds.

x

As we waded through the high sedge growth and sloppy water, wetting the backs of our legs just below the knees— for in wading over these quaking bogs the back of the knee-joint is the part that bears the brunt,—we came across one or two rail-runs, but no more, for the water-rail is becoming very scarce.

After we had waded through the marshy crop, we entered the tall reed-beds, where the air was hot and moist, and the reed-tassels cut one's face, and shivered and waved in the rising breeze—all the reeds melting in a formless, shimmering, amber waste, that glimmered and glowed against the pale ground. Only the open sky over our heads was quiet; after a time this reed intoxication passed off, and one could watch the sedge- and reed-warblers courting.

And we broke like wild animals from the hot reed brake, the perspiration pouring from our faces, and the midges, that fortunately were scarce, biting us, glad to feel *en plein air* again.

LXV

POLLY'S VALENTINE

ACK WELTON'S day had come, and little Polly Rose sat eagerly, in the little brick-floored room, looking at the great china dogs on the mantelpiece as if they were household gods.

Rap, rap! knocked Jack Welton, and Polly ran to the door, and her little heart gave a bound as she picked up a bright piece of red ribbon. It was just such a piece as she had longed for to bind across the black coils of hair that waved on her olive temples; for Polly was dark-skinned, like the children of the South.

Knock, knock! again rapped the nimble Jack Welton, and Polly dropped her ribbon and ran to the door. When she lifted the latch her bright black eyes danced with pleasure, for a nice pinafore, gay with blue ribbons, lay on the clean, freshly-sanded, red bricks. Polly had just put on the dainty pinafore and bound her temples with the silken fillet when *rap, rap!* again knocked Jack Welton at the door.

to the door and opened it. Something flashed across the sunlight, and little Polly forgot her ruddy fillet and her pretty pinafore; her whole being seemed to have received a shock; the world had vanished from her, and seemed to be slipping away, away into the darkness down a deep abyss

. . . Then she seemed to awake and to hear distant voices, and suddenly she knew she had received a terrible blow in one of her black eyes; and little by little, as the bright world came back to her, she recalled how she had opened the door and saw little John Read throw a stone at her. She remembered, too, the flash of the smooth pebble athwart the sunlight; and now she realised it all, and, putting her hand up to her face she felt a bandage over her right eye, and she felt that she would never see the bright world again through that eye. Big tears started into her eyes, and she looked down and saw a few spots of blood upon the pinafore given her on that bright day, and her little heart was wellnigh broken

. . The villagers had collected money, and four months afterwards little Polly was playing Scotch-hop one June by the dusty hedge, white with honeysuckle, when Annie Wynne asked her to show her her glass eye

Polly stopped, and the children gathered round eagerly as she deftly took out the coloured glass globe, placing it in little Annie's brown hand. Annie gazed upon the china, black and white, until a shout from a drover startled her, as some wild Irish cattle dashed up the road, raising dust-particles that gleamed in the fierce sunlight

The children screamed and ran up into the hedge, and Annie dropped and lost the glass eye ; and Polly now goes to school with a green shade over her sightless globe, hoping that Jack Welton will bring her a new eye next Valentine's Day, when she will be again known amongst the school-children as 'one eye and a peppermint.'

Lightning Source UK Ltd.
Milton Keynes UK
UKOW020744021212

203059UK00005B/201/P